Camping Guide to Kenya

Camping Guide to
Kenya

**1990
Edition**

David Else

Illustrations by Jill Bitten

BRADT PUBLICATIONS, UK
HUNTER PUBLISHING, USA

First published in 1989 by Bradt Publications, 41 Nortoft Rd, Chalfont St Peter, Bucks SL9 0LA, England. Distributed in the USA by Hunter Publishing Inc., 300 Rariton Center Parkway, CN94, Edison, NJ 08818.

Second updated printing, March 1990.

British Library Cataloguing in Publication Data
Else, David
  Camping guide to Kenya.
  1. Kenya. Visitors' guides
  I. Title
  916.76'2044

ISBN 0-946983-31-3

Photos by the authors.
Cover photos: Reticulated giraffes in Samburu Reserve (H. Bradt). Yare Safaris campsite, Maralal. Mount Kenya (photo courtesy of Ultimate Equipment Ltd).

Phototypeset from Authors' disk by Saxon Printing Ltd, Derby, England.

Printed and bound in Great Britain by
The Guernsey Press Co. Ltd., Guernsey, Channel Islands.

THANKS

During our time in Kenya, researching for this book, we received a great deal of help from various people. We would particularly like to thank Ben Rode and Nancy O'Donnel, Richard Mandel and Nanna Bo Christensen, Mike Wylie and Marie-Louise Boley, Mike and Linda Garner, Mike Lawrence, Richard and Laurie Goldsmith, Njagi Gakungu (Uvambuzi Club), Paul Clarke (Mountain Club of Kenya), Alan Dixson (Let's Go Travel), Solomon Muangi (Intermediate Technology), and Joy Belsky (Tsavo Savanah Project).

For help of a different sort, some kind of mention should also go to the members of Nairobi Hash House Harriers; On-On!

Last, but by no means least, for a hot shower, cold beer, and juggling to 'The Joshua Tree', an extra special thank-you to Mike Wood and Sheila Copeland.

We would also like to express our gratitude to the staff of the Kenyan Embassy in London, and to Mr Musila, the Director of Tourism at the Ministry of Wildlife and Tourism in Nairobi.

CONTRIBUTORS

For additional information and contributions the following people also deserve to see their names in print:
Sabine Tamm, Matthew Roundtree, Arik Orbach, Limor Rozen, Ady and Dudy, Godwin Kagumba, Kevin Bishop, Lauraine Merlini, Alistair and Pauline Taylor, Dianne Bibby, Reinhold Scharf, John and Jenny Edwards, John Arkle, Linda Brown, John Kerrin, Elizabeth Slinn, John Simmons, Florence Williams, Gerhard Bronner, Jude Granger, Eileen King, Edward Kahindi, Andrew Rzewuzku, Owen Sumbu (Kitale Museum), Lionel Nutter, Diana Tangui, Enid Kaplan and Jordan Deitcher, Joan Mayer, Jane Dalrymple, Alan Graham, Mrs J Barnley, Peg Bitten, Jiko, Sharon Newcombe, Joseph Flaherty, Richard Lewis, Louise Harvey, Jim Taylor, David from Murang'a, and Hazey the elephant man.

BE A CONTRIBUTOR!

This book was updated by David and Jill following a three month return visit to Kenya in 1989/90. If you have any new information you feel should be added, please write to us at Bradt Publications (the address is on the facing page).

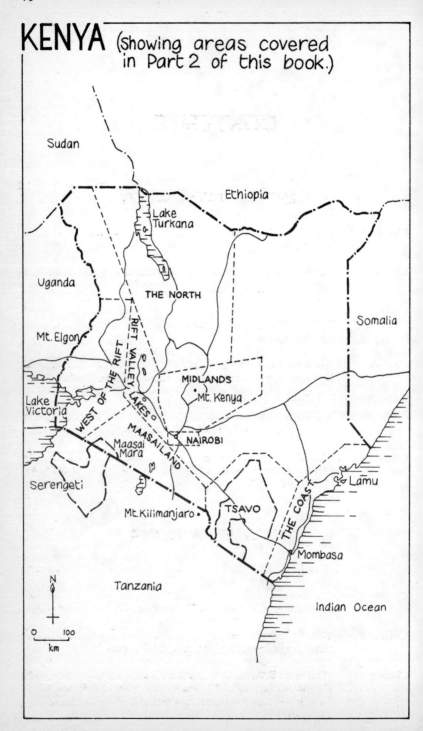

KENYA (showing areas covered in Part 2 of this book.)

Sudan

Ethiopia

Lake Turkana

Uganda

THE NORTH

Mt. Elgon

Somalia

RIFT VALLEY

WEST OF THE RIFT

LAKES

MIDLANDS

Mt. Kenya

Lake Victoria

MAASAILAND

NAIROBI

Maasai Mara

Serengeti

Mt. Kilimanjaro

TSAVO

THE COAST

Lamu

Mombasa

N

Tanzania

Indian Ocean

0   100
km

CONTENTS

GENERAL INFORMATION

Chapter 1   **Camping in Kenya** 1
When to go 2.

Chapter 2   **Getting There** 3
Flying direct 3, Overland from Europe 4.

Chapter 3   **Preparations** 7
Entry requirements 7, Vaccinations 7, Financial matters 8,
Reading up 10.

Chapter 4   **Getting Around** 11
Self-drive cars 11, Camping safari companies 14, Public
transport 17, Hitch-hiking 18, Walking & cycling 19.

Chapter 5   **Equipment and Provisions** 21
Tents 22, Sleeping 26, Cooking 27, Rucksacks 32, Clothes 33.

Chapter 6   **Miscellaneous Information** 35
National parks & reserves 35, Coast 38, Health 39, Security 40,
Natural history 42, Books 44, Maps 49, Glossary 52, Key to
maps 53.

CAMPSITES IN KENYA

Chapter 7   **Nairobi** 55

Chapter 8   **Maasailand** 63
Maasai Mara 65, Amboseli 71, Namanga 74, Olorgasailie 75.

Chapter 9   **The Rift Valley Lakes** 77
Naivasha 79, Nakuru 83, Bogoria 85, Baringo 88.

Chapter 10   **West of the Rift** 91
Kisumu 92, Londiani 94, Siaya 97, Kakamega 98, Eldoret &
area 101, Kitale & area 102, Cherangani Hills 104, Mount
Elgon 107.

Chapter 11 **The Midlands** **117**
Mount Kenya 120, Aberdare 129, Ol Doinyo Sapuk 133,
Nyahururu 135, Nanyuki area 137, Meru 141.

Chapter 12 **The North** **145**
Lake Turkana west 146, Maralal 148, Road to east Turkana
150, Loyangalani 152, Mathews Range 154, Samburu &
Buffalo Springs 157, Marsabit 161, Sibiloi 163.

Chapter 13 **Tsavo** **167**
Tsavo west 169, Tsavo east 173, Tsavo area 176.

Chapter 14 **The Coast** **179**
Mombasa 180, North of Mombasa 183, Malindi 186, Lamu 189,
South of Mombasa 191, Wasini 194, Shimba Hills 197.

In Amboseli National Park.

Chapter 1

Camping In Kenya

Kenya is one of the most popular tourist destinations in Africa. Every year hundreds of thousands of visitors come to Kenya: to see huge herds of wild animals roaming free in the national parks, to enjoy the sun, sand and surf on the palm-lined Indian Ocean coast, or to climb the famous snow-capped mountain peaks that straddle the equator.

In this one country, the visitor can travel through an astoundingly wide variety of landscapes: from desert plains, through lush grassland and dense forest to high mountain moorlands or tropical coastline. And travelling with a tent is, without a doubt, the best way for visitors to experience the sights and attractions that Kenya has to offer.

Put briefly; a tent gives you freedom, independence, and flexibility.

In the popular areas you do not have to rely on expensive and frequently overbooked hotels and lodges. In the less visited regions a tent means you can travel confidently with no worries about finding accommodation at the end of the day. With a tent you can easily escape from the crowds, and completely self-contained campers can travel as far away from the tourist centres, and the rest of civilisation, as time and inclination allow.

When camping you are immediately closer to your surroundings; you become a part of the environment rather than a mere observer. This is the genuine African safari experience that first attracted explorers, hunters and pioneers, and in these more recent times has a similar appeal for tourists and travellers with a taste for adventure who come to Kenya armed with nothing more than a zoom lens. It is a sense of oneness with the wild which always arouses such remarkable sensations – a mixture of peace and tranquillity edged with excitement or a hint of danger. Nothing can compare with the emotions felt when sitting round a good campfire under a starry African sky, as a lion roars in the distance...

Camping provides something for everybody in Kenya. Organised campsites range from fully equipped sites with all facilities, including showers, bar and swimming pool, to very basic patches of ground in isolated spots which are so rarely used that you will probably have to clear the long grass yourself before pitching your tent.

There are also endless possibilities for unofficial, or 'wild' camping. Although Kenya is a developed nation by African standards, vast areas of the country still remain unexploited and seldom visited by tourists, giving intrepid campers a virtually unlimited choice of places to camp. Even in populated areas, where tourists are an uncommon sight, 'enterprise' camping is usually possible at a variety of unofficial locations such as schools, church missions, scout camps, and even police stations. You usually only have to ask and you will find most people are happy to help.

Campers who prefer to be completely independent will drive to the various official and wild sites, or travel by public transport and hitch-hiking, carrying all that is needed on the roof-rack or in a rucksack. Alternatively, professional companies based in Kenya, Europe or North America, organise camping safaris which can cut most of the logistical worries, especially for first time visitors or those with limited time.

WHEN TO GO

Kenya's wide variety of landscape types means that the country experiences a wide variety of climatic patterns. Generally speaking the rainy periods are March to May ('the long rains') and November to December ('the short rains'). From June to October the weather is warm and dry, while January to February is the hottest and driest time of the year. Rainfall is also affected by local factors. In northern desert regions the rainy seasons are very short and sometimes non-existent. On the coast and in the mountains rainfall is higher.

Generally, during rainy seasons, the mornings are dry and the rain tends to fall during the afternoon or evening.

Tourist seasons follow climatic patterns and most visitors come during the dry periods as travel is easier and animals are more readily viewed at this time. However, although campers can always escape the crowds (even in the popular months), Kenya is worth visiting out of the tourist season. During the last month of the long rains the landscape is at its greenest and most beautiful. Also at this time of year official campsites are likely to be less crowded, while hotels and lodges often make significant price reductions.

Hire-cars and organised camping safaris are usually much cheaper in the low season too, and at all Kenya's tourist spots you will generally find the atmosphere more relaxed and the people more friendly than at the height of the season.

Chapter 2

Getting There

FLYING DIRECT

From Europe

Flights to Nairobi are available from a number of European cities including Athens, Frankfurt and Amsterdam, but the level of competition and the discount fares offered by many specialist travel agents often means that London is one of the cheapest places to buy a ticket.

British Airways and Kenya Airways offer direct London − Nairobi flights which do not involve changing planes. Other airlines with services between London and Nairobi include Aeroflot, Air France, Egypt Air, Ethiopian Airways, Gulf Air, KLM, Lufthansa, Olympic Airways, PanAm, Sabena, Saudia, Air Sudan, and Swissair. The quality of service, frequency of flights, departure and arrival times, and (of course) the fares offered by these airlines vary greatly. Other factors affecting the price include the length of return (ie: the amount of time you plan to spend in Kenya), and whether the ticket is fixed dated or open ended (ie: if you have to return on a certain date).

When shopping around for a flight, to save contacting all these airlines direct, use a specialist travel agent who can find the cheapest flight, or the one that best suits your requirements.

Africa Travel Centre (ATC), 4 Medway Court, Leigh St, London WC1H 9QX, Tel: 01 387 1211, are specialists in African destinations including Nairobi, and also offer a range of small-group or self-drive safaris in Kenya.

STA Travel, 117 Euston Rd, London NW1, Tel: 01 581 1022, have their own Africa Desk (01 388 2266) with experienced staff dealing specifically with flights to Kenya and other African destinations.

Trailfinders, 42−48 Earls Court Rd, Kensington, London W8 6EJ, Tel: 01 938 3366, offer a wide range of flights to Nairobi and other African destinations, and also have an excellent back-up service for travellers, with a library and information centre, a vaccination service, and a worldwide discount scheme for transcontinental passengers.

Alternatively, scan the advertisements on the travel pages of the quality daily and Sunday papers to see if there are any special deals available. In London *Time Out*, *TNT Magazine* and *Trailfinder* are also a good source of information.

From the USA

Most flights to East Africa from America are from New York. Visitors to Kenya flying from the States with limited time to spare use PanAm's direct New York – Nairobi flight. Zambia Airways also fly this route at a cheaper rate, via Lusaka. Other travellers with a little more time fly to London, or another European capital, and then buy a ticket to Nairobi there. This works out cheaper, but unless you plan to tie in Europe as part of wider travels, this might mean waiting until a flight is arranged.

It is also possible for people outside the UK to reserve and pay for their London – Nairobi ticket in advance by contacting one of the agents listed above. Tickets will still have to be collected in London as they cannot be legally sent across international borders.

STA have offices in various US cities. Their NY address is Suite 800, 17 E. 45 St., NY 10017. Tel: 212 986 9470. Access International have also been recommended for cheap flights from New York to Africa. They often advertise in the New York Times. Their address is 250 West 57 Street, New York, NY.

From Australasia

Like flights from the USA, those to Nairobi direct from Australia are infrequent and expensive, so many travellers with time to spare fly to London and pick up a cheaper ticket there. One alternative is to fly via Bangkok, Delhi or Bombay. Another, suitable for overland travellers planning to take in other East African countries as part of their journey, is the Quantas flight from Sydney to Harare in Zimbabwe.

OVERLAND FROM EUROPE

Independent Travellers

For overland travellers in Africa, Kenya is a natural and practical destination. The traditional 'Nile Route' to Kenya from Egypt through Sudan has been off-limits to travellers since the outbreak of civil war in southern Sudan in 1983. This overland route to Kenya now involves travelling from Sudan through Central African Republic, Zaire, and Uganda or Tanzania. An alternative route avoids Sudan altogether, crossing the Sahara from Algeria to Niger and approaching CAR via Chad, or Nigeria, and Cameroon.

Intrepid independent overlanders can reach Kenya this way, driving their own vehicle or travelling by public transport and hitching, but these routes are long and arduous, and not to be approached lightly. Travellers with vehicles should be aware of the long distances, rough terrain and limited mechanical assistance available in case of emergency, and prepare their vehicles accordingly. For information on these routes read, *The Trans Saharan Handbook*, *Backpacker's Africa (West and Central)*, and *Africa on a Shoestring*. (For full details of all the books mentioned in this guide see the *Guide Books* section on page 44.)   For information about overland camping vehicles contact Overland Ltd, 31B, West Wilts Trading Estate, Westbury, Wiltshire, UK, Tel: (0373) 858272.

Overland Tours

If you have no great time restrictions (and especially if it is your first visit to Africa) various UK based companies organise overland tours from London to Nairobi in specially converted four-wheel-drive trucks. These overland tour companies provide an interesting and inexpensive way of getting to Kenya. Even if you intend to go it alone once you arrive in Kenya, joining an overland truck is a useful introduction to African ways. The driver/tour leader is familiar with routes and towns along the way, and can cope with border crossings, road blocks and other potential difficulties. Disadvantages include a pre-planned, fairly rigid, itinerary and spending several weeks with other travellers who may not be compatible.

Most of these overland tour companies also run camping safaris inside Kenya, or on to other East African countries from Nairobi. These safaris can be booked in advance before you leave for Kenya, which is useful for visitors with limited time who want to combine an organised safari with their own independent travels.

Many overland companies advertise in travel magazines or the travel sections of national newspapers, or are represented by specialist travel agents such as those mentioned above. These include: *Exodus*, All Saints Passage, 100 Wandsworth High Street, London SW18, UK, Tel: (01) 870 0151; *Guerba Expeditions*, 101 Eden Vale Road, Westbury, Wiltshire, UK, (0800) 373334; *Hobo Trans Africa*, Wisset Place, Halesworth, Suffolk, UK, Tel: (09867) 3124; *Kumuka Africa*, 141a Kensington High Street, London W8, UK, Tel: (01) 938 2973; *Tracks Africa*, 12 Abingdon Road, London W8, UK, (01) 937 3028.

Chapter 3

Preparations

ENTRY REQUIREMENTS

All visitors to Kenya require a full passport. A temporary passport is not enough even if you plan a short stay in Kenya. Check that your passport will not expire during your visit, although renewal at most embassies is usually a fairly straightforward process.

Visas are required by citizens of most countries accept those from the United Kingdom, Ireland, West Germany, Netherlands, Spain and Turkey. If you come from one of these countries a Visitors Pass will be issued at your point of entry, allowing a three month stay (usually renewable). For other nationalities visas should be obtained before arrival. Visas are not available at airports or borders.

You may have to show vaccination certificates for cholera and yellow fever when you enter Kenya, and have a return, or onward, air ticket to prove you can leave. If you do not have an air ticket you may be asked to show 'sufficient funds'. This should be around St 250 or US$ 400, but tends to vary, so an international credit card is useful to show you have access to more money if necessary.

Visas and more information about entry requirements can be obtained from a Kenyan embassy or high commission.

VACCINATIONS

All visitors to Kenya must be vaccinated for cholera and yellow fever. Vaccinations are also usually recommended for typhoid, tetanus, and hepatitis A. Remember that some vaccinations require a course of injections over many weeks, so don't leave everything until the last minute. Make sure that your doctor is well informed about current recommendations, or contact one of the specialist vaccination information centres listed below to get detailed and up-to-date advice.

The Ross Institute of Tropical Hygiene
London School of Hygiene and Tropical Medicine
Keppel Street (off Gower Street)
London WC1E 7HT, Tel: 01 636 8636.

The Malarial Reference Laboratory is located here. A continuous loop tape provides general information on 01 636 7921. For enquiries telephone 01 636 3924, 0930–1030 h, 1400–1500 h, Monday – Friday.

The Medical Advisory Service for Travellers Abroad (MASTA) can provide a comprehensive Health Brief to suit individual requirements. A fee is made for this service. For more information contact MASTA at the London School of Hygiene and Tropical medicine, or telephone 01 631 4408.

The Hospital for Tropical Hygiene
4 St Pancras Way, London NW1 0PE, Tel: 01 387 4411.

Liverpool School of Tropical Medicine
Pembroke Place, Liverpool L3 5QA, Tel: 051 708 9393.

The immunisation centre at Trailfinders, 42–48 Earls Court Rd, London W8 6EJ, is open 1000–1300 h, 1330–1630 h Monday – Friday. No appointment is necessary, and Trailfinders clients qualify for reduced fees. Telephone 01 938 3444.

British Airways Travel Clinics are located in various cities in the UK. Using information from MASTA, up-dated daily, these clinics provide information and advice about travellers' health requirements. All vaccinations and immunisations are available, without a further appointment being necessary. For more information, and the position of your nearest Travel Clinic, telephone 01 430 0027.

Thomas Cook Vaccination Centre, 45 Berkeley St, London W1A 1EB, Tel: 01 499 4000.

The International Association of Medical Assistance to Travellers produces a booklet with innoculation and general health information for people travelling and working overseas. Ask your doctor or a vaccination centre for details.

For more information read *The Traveller's Health Guide* or *Travellers' Health*. Full details in *Suggested Reading*.

FINANCIAL MATTERS

Money

Kenya's unit of currency is the Kenya shilling (written KSh or /–, and often called a bob), divided into 100 cents. In 1990 the rate of exchange was US$1 = 22/-, St£1 = 36/-, DM = 13/-. This is likely to change, but generally as prices rise, so do exchange rates, making the cost to visitors about the same. Prices in this book are quoted in shillings, mostly at the 1988 rate, and even if prices do rise they will be useful as comparisons.

For tourists, US dollars or sterling pounds are the easiest to change into Kenyan currency. Travellers cheques are best for security but difficult to cash outside main towns. An internationally known brand of travellers cheque is more readily accepted. Contact your bank for more details.

An unofficial, or black, market exists for hard currency in Kenya, usually a few shillings more than the official rate. If you decide to change on the blackmarket remember that you are depriving a developing country of its major source of foreign exchange, and, more importantly, that blackmarket dealing is highly illegal, and can be very dangerous. Never change on the street and beware of con-men and police agents.

In remote areas small change is always in short supply. Carry a good supply of small denomination notes when on safari to avoid being short changed.

In Kenya the distinction between a tip and a bribe is less distinct than in the West. Many officials or workers may expect extra payment for carrying out their duties. To pay encourages the continuation of this system, not to pay may cause delays or difficulties. Use your judgement.

Costs

The cost of your trip depends very much on your standard of travel.

If you camp in official campsites every night allow 35/– per night. For the times when camping is not possible; basic lodgings can be found for around 50/– per night, a double room in a mid-range hotel for 250/–, in a good quality hotel or lodge for 900/–, and in the Nairobi Hilton for 2,500/–.

Hitch-hiking is generally free, and for public transport allow approximately 1/– for every 1 –2 km on the bus, more in shared taxis. Car hire costs vary considerably between companies and models. Hiring a Suzuki Sierra, the most reasonably priced 4WD car available, costs between 400 – 500/- per day (about St£13 – 17 or US$20 – 25) plus between 5 – 6/– per km (20p/30c). Hired for a whole week with no kilometre charge costs between 8,500 – 12,500/– (St280 – 400 or US$450 – 600). Petrol in Kenya costs about 10/– per litre, and on an average safari, combining tarred and dirt road driving, Suzukis do about 10km to the litre.

Cheap restaurants, or *hotelis* (see the glossary on page 52 for an explanation of all Kenyan Swahili terms) have basic snacks for 5/–, and reasonable meals can be bought in Nairobi restaurants for between 30 – 100/– . International style meals in hotels and lodges start at around 300/– per course.

Independent campers should remember to include national park and reserve entrance fees (see the *National Parks and Reserves* section in Chapter 6).

An organised camping safari will also add to your overall costs. Although prices and standards vary considerably, some good value companies operate trips at prices cheaper than you could do it yourself. For more details see the *Camping Safari Companies* section.

So many variables are involved when camping in Kenya, that giving an approximate daily cost could be misleading. This is why the more detailed cost breakdowns are given above. But as a guide, travellers on the tightest budget could survive on £3/$5 per day, while mid-range travellers could relax on £10/$17 − £15/$25 per day. This covers food and accommodation only; costs for public transport, car hire, park entrance fees, and beer will be different for everybody and should be added.

Insurance

For visitors to Kenya, insurance is highly recommended. Conditions in local hospitals are often poor, and private hospitals are expensive. If you are ill or have an accident your insurance should cover all medical costs, including emergency air evacuation (inside Kenya as well as from Kenya to your home country) if necessary, and stolen belongings.

STA, Trailfinders and the Africa Travel Centre (addresses in *Getting There*) all offer insurance policies designed for overseas travel. Check which company offer the policy and price best suited to your requirements.

In Kenya, tourists can become temporary members of the Flying Doctors' Society. In case of serious illness or injury you will be provided with emergency treatment and air transport. If not used your money goes towards the Flying Doctor Service of The African Medical and Research Foundation which assists various East African governments with their medical programmes, particularly in rural areas. Membership costs US$20 per year, tourist membership S$10 per month. For more details contact The Flying Doctors' Society of Africa, PO Box 30125, Nairobi, Tel: 501300/1/2/3 or 500508. The society's offices are in the AMREF building at Wilson Airport. The phone number in the U.K. is (0272) 238424/5.

Air Africa Rescue (Kenya) Ltd also offer air rescues and complete medical cover in case of emergency. Annual subscription costs 4,380/−. For further details contact AAR, PO Box 41766, Nairobi, Tel: 337030, 337306, 337432, 337504. The company's office is in Uganda House, Baring Arcade, Kenyatta Avenue, Nairobi.

If you are unable to arrange insurance before arriving in Kenya, temporary travel insurance can be arranged with Alico (The American Life Insurance Company). For more details contact an insurance agent or Alico direct at PO Box 30364, Nairobi.

READING UP

An important aspect of your preparations before coming to Kenya should be to find out as much as you can about the country. Try a few novels or travel books to get yourself in the mood, and scan the foreign pages of newspapers to find out what is happening on the political and current affairs front. In this way when you arrive you will not suffer so much from culture shock, and can be more aware of what is going on around you.

Chapter 4

Getting Around

SELF-DRIVE CARS

Hiring a car (or using your own if you are a resident or citizen) gives you the freedom to drive anywhere, as and when you please. You are not tied to public transport timetables (where they exist!) or forced to rely on hitch-hiking. A four wheel drive (4WD) vehicle with a high and low ratio gearbox means you can leave the tarred roads behind, and will increase your range and possibilities even further. If you want to visit the national parks independently, a car is not essential, but it certainly makes things much easier.

For travellers on a budget the cost of hiring a car can be a limiting factor, although this can be reduced considerably when shared between three or four people. People with spare seats or looking for companions will advertise around Nairobi. Look at the notice boards at the budget hotels, at the youth hostel, or in the Thorn Tree Cafe.

When hiring a car look carefully at what the various companies have to offer. Remember to take into account the charges per day and per kilometre, any insurance costs, and the deposit (a credit card payment is usually acceptable). Also ask about the collision damage waiver (CDW) which exempts you from any costs in case of an accident caused by a third party. Even with a CDW you may be liable for a certain amount in case of an accident. Good companies will charge a reasonable sum, between 2000 and 5000/-, while other less reputable companies may try to charge up to 20,000/-. This makes the CDW almost pointless and could be very expensive for you in the event of an accident.

Other questions to ask when hiring a car include: Does the company have its own fleet of cars or do they sub-hire? Is the company they sub-hire from reputable? What is the back up service in case of accident or breakdown? Can they give professional advice on roads or reliable garages *en route*? What items will you be liable for in case of theft (eg spare wheel, tools)? Is the windscreen covered against accidental breakage?

The following car-hire companies can be recommended.

Hertz, UTC Ltd, PO Box 42196, corner of Kaunda and Muindi Mbingu Streets, Nairobi, Tel: 331960, have a full range of 4WD and saloon cars available at daily or weekly rates,and also rent fully-equipped vehicles for self-drive camping safaris at a separate daily rate (unlimited distance).

Budget Rent-a-Car, PO Box 59767, corner of Parliament Lane and Haile Selassie Avenue, Nairobi, Tel: 23304, 24081, 337154, 330169.

Concorde Car Hire, PO Box 25053, Agip Petrol Station, Wyaki Way, near Westlands Roundabout, Nairobi, Tel: 743008, 743011.

Coast Car Hire, PO Box 56707, Standard Street, near New Stanley Hotel, Nairobi, Tel: 20365, 336570.

Let's Go Travel, PO Box 60342, Standard Street, near the main Post Office (GPO), Nairobi, Tel: 29539, 29540, 340331.

These companies can all provide 4WD cars (usually Suzuki Sierras, or something similar), and if you have not brought all your own gear, any extra camping equipment (tents, sleeping bags, jerry cans, tables, lamps, cool boxes, etc) can be hired at extra cost on request. Most car-hire companies also have saloon cars and large powerful 4WD vehicles available if required.

Habib's Car Hire, PO Box 48095, Agip House, Haile Selassie Avenue, Nairobi, Tel: 20463, 23816, 20985, rent unique camper-vehicles with folding tents mounted on the roof which are easy to put up, high enough to catch cool night breezes, and give an instant vantage point when you wake up in the morning. A complete set of camping equipment is supplied with each camper.

Hertz and Budget cars can be reserved in advance through their international networks. The Africa Travel Centre (see address in *Getting There*) can also arrange hire-cars ready for collection as part of their *Self Drive Discoverer* service.

Costs involved in hiring a car vary considerably between companies. For a brief outline see the *Costs* section in Chapter 3.

Buying a car

For most tourists in Kenya, buying a car involves a lot of money and paperwork. Even secondhand cars are not cheap (15,000/– for a Suzuki Sierra). Duty would not have to be paid if the car was bought and sold inside Kenya, but registration tax, road tax (600/– for three months), and insurance (around 10,000/– per year for a driver with good no-claims certificates) all need to be taken into account. Re-selling a car is difficult, leaving you with large amounts of Kenyan currency. Selling for foreign currency is illegal.

Cars are advertised for sale in the daily newspapers, and a weekly sale takes place in the car park of the Sarit Shopping Centre in Westlands every Sunday.

The only legal way to buy a car is to import the necessary foreign currency, change it into Kenyan shillings at a bank, keeping all the receipts. When you re-sell the car you should be able to change the Kenyan currency back into pounds or dollars. That's the theory...

Various illegal ways around this problem do exist, but these often lead to their own problems.

Legal conditions

No special licence is required to drive cars in Kenya. A visitors' own licence is acceptable for periods up to 90 days, but it must be endorsed at a police station in Kenya. Your car hire company will advise on this. An international drivers licence is easily available from national driving organisations (the AA in Britain) and does not need endorsing.

Visitors bringing vehicles into Kenya with registrations other than Kenyan, Ugandan or Tanzanian must get an Internal Circulation Permit from the Licencing Officer in Nairobi. This is issued free on production of *carnet*, customs duty receipt, and certificate of insurance. Your own national motoring organisation, or the AA in Kenya will be able to give further information.

Road conditions

The roads between main towns are usually tarred and in fairly good condition although some stretches can be badly potholed. While you have to be on your guard for people and livestock walking on the roads, your main concern will be other drivers. The standard of driving in Kenya is not high; lorry and bus drivers can be particularly dangerous. Car drivers should be constantly alert for blind overtaking, sudden turns, and vehicles switching carriageways to avoid potholes. The accident rate in towns, and on the open road, is appallingly high. Extra care should be taken at night.

Driving off road is considerably slower and more wearing for driver and vehicle, but is probably safer than on busy tarred roads. Many roads are graded dirt (*murram*) and in good condition, while others are badly potholed or corrugated. Resist temptation to drive too fast on dirt roads, it is easy to skid on the loose surface, leave the road and end up rolling your vehicle.

The speed limit on main roads is 80 kph, in towns 50 kph, and on dirt roads 30 kph. When estimating journey times allow 60 km per hour on tarred roads and 20 km per hour on dirt.

Sun glasses are very useful against direct sunlight or glare, and sitting on a towel when travelling in warm conditions makes for a more comfortable drive.

When leaving the car, lock all windows and doors. In towns keep the car in view, or do not leave any baggage in an unattended car. If you have to leave the car in a town it may be worth paying a guard (20/– for a couple of hours). Beware of bogus mechanics finding 'faults' in your car at petrol stations. They pick on hire cars as drivers often presume the company will pay for any repairs. This has happened at Nakuru, Isiolo and some other towns. Some of these con-men even go as far as putting a real fault on your car while you are not watching.

CAMPING SAFARI COMPANIES

In recent years new laws have restricted the building of hotels and lodges in Kenya's national parks. This has led to an increase in the number of tented camps (permanently pitched luxury tents, hardly discernable from a solid lodge, and not covered in this book), and in the number of organised camping safaris.

Many visitors find that these organised safaris provide a useful introduction, giving them a feel of camping in Kenya before venturing out on their own. The various companies based in and around Nairobi offer a wide selection of camping safaris, ranging from a quick visit to Amboseli, or another easily accessible park, through ten day hauls to Lake Turkana, to two weeks luxury private camps in Shaba or Maasai Mara. Companies use either minibuses (sometimes called *combis*, but nothing like VW vans), Landrovers, Landcruisers, or specially converted trucks. Tents range from compact lightweights to large traditional canvas frame tents.

Naturally the costs involved vary considerably too. As a very rough guide budget companies usually charge around $50/£30 per day for short (3 day) trips. The daily rate usually decreases as the length of the trip increases; a 10 day budget trip costs around $25/£15 per day. Mid-range companies charge around $150—250 per day, and top of the range full luxury safaris are often in the $500 per day range. Generally speaking, you get what you pay for, so you should always take the best you can afford.

Although most of the camping safari companies are reputable and experienced, a number of unscrupulous outfits operate badly organised, under-equipped tours led by inexperienced guides. Check that the vehicles are properly licenced to operate safaris. PSV (Public Service Vehicle) and RSL (Road Service Licence) stickers should be visible on the windscreen.

It is worth noting that even with the most reputable company your safari may be affected by unavoidable breakdowns or other delays caused by bad roads or communication difficulties.

Ask also about the tour and its transport. Some companies run large 24—seater buses where only some of the windows open making game photography difficult. Other companies have minibuses or Landrovers with pop-up roofs offering a 360 degree viewpoint. Does the company have its own vehicles or does it sub-hire? Do the vehicles carry spares? Are the drivers and cooks experienced, long-term employees of the company, or inexperienced casual staff? Will the tour keep to an itinerary? What refunds will be available if any part of the tour is missed due to breakdown etc?

Ask about the equipment. What condition is it in? How often is it replaced? How big (and therefore how comfortable) are the tents? What equipment is provided, and what should passengers bring?

Some companies will pass your booking on to another company if they do not fill all their places. Check if this is going to happen and ask the same questions about the sub-contracted company. It is also worth asking if your tour is complete, or if you are joining the second part of a longer safari. It can be annoying if you want to stop to take pictures of game that other passengers have already seen and photographed satisfactorily.

Even if you are on a tight budget, do not go straight for the cheapest company. You might miss an excellent safari, all for the sake of saving a couple of hundred bob. It is best, if you can, to speak to other tourists and travellers for recommendations and comments. However, the companies listed below (all with offices in central Nairobi) can be recommended.

Several companies in Kenya operate at the very top of the range, offering personally led, exclusive, luxury camping safaris, specially tailored to suit individual requirements. Two such companies are:

Mike Garner Safaris, PO Box 15030. Tel: 882216.

Westminster Safaris, PO Box 57046, Westminster House, Kenyatta Ave. Tel: 338041, 338045, 29161.

Bushbuck Adventures Ltd, PO Box 67449, Gilfillan House, Kenyatta Ave, Tel: 60437, 728737, run scheduled camping safaris to the Maasai Mara, Tsavo and other popular parks, and also organise special walking safaris in the Aberdare Mountains and on Mount Kenya and Mount Elgon. Information from Wildlife Safaris, 26 Newnham Green, Maldon, Essex, CM9 6HZ, Great Britain. Tel: (0621) 53172.

Other specialised camping safari companies include:

Executive Wilderness Programmes, PO Box 44827. Tel: 60728, or 32 Seamill Park Crescent, Worthing, BN11 2PN, Great Britain.

Tropical Ice Ltd, PO Box 57341. Tel 740811 (walking and mountain trekking).

Safaris Unlimited, PO Box 20138. Tel: 332132 (Horseback camping safaris).

Zirkuli Expeditions, PO Box 34548. Tel: 23949, 20848 (Motorbike camping safaris).

A new company offering camping safaris by vehicle or mountain bike is Great Expectations Ltd, Protection House, Corner of Parliament Rd and Haile Selassie Ave, Nairobi, PO Box 10788; Tel: 26770, Fax 26584.

Companies offering budget camping safaris to all parts of Kenya include:

Special Camping Safaris, PO Box 51512, Gilfillan House, Kenyatta Avenue. Tel: 338325, 882541.

Gametrackers, PO Box 62042, Banda Street, between Koinange and Loita Streets. Tel: 338927, 22703, 504281.

Safari Seekers, PO Box 32347, Jubilee Insurance Exchange, Kaunda Street. Tel: 26206, 334585.

Safari Camp Services, PO Box 44801, corner of Koinange and Moktar Daddah Streets. Tel: 28936, 330130.

For Gametrackers, Special Camping, and Safari Camp Services, bookings for safaris can be made in advance from abroad, but visitors are welcome at the companies' offices and can reserve space with any camping safari on the spot. Safari Camp Services also offer mid-range *Authentic* and up-market *Luxury* camping safaris, as well as their now legendary Turkana Bus which has been operating continuously for over eleven years. They are also an agency for budget hire cars and can provide a complete Rent-a-Tent box of camping equipment for visitors who want to safari independently.

For something different, Yare Safaris run camping safaris from Nairobi and from their hostel and campsite at Maralal (see page 149). Yare Safaris also organise transport between Nairobi and Maralal and are the only company in Nairobi running overland camping safaris into Zaire to see the mountain gorillas. For more information contact Yare Safaris, PO Box 63006, Nairobi; Tel: 559313 or visit their office on the corner of Melili and Mukenia Roads, in Nairobi South C, a suburban area to the left (north- east) side of the main Mombasa road beyond the Nyayo Stadium (30 minutes walk from Kenyatta Ave).

When looking for your camping safari, check that the company you go with is a member of KATO, the Kenyan Association of Tour Operators. Members of this government recognised body have to fulfill certain guidelines laid down by the KATO Ethics and Standards Committee, and if necessary the Association will take up a complaint about one of its members.

Avoid booking a safari through one of the many agents who sell on the street. If anything goes wrong the company concerned may well refuse to co-operate and refer you back to the agent, who will inevitably be difficult or impossible to find again.

If time is limited and you are unable to shop around the various camping safari companies, many travel agents in central Nairobi can book a trip with a particular company to suit your requirements. However, not all agents represent a comprehensive selection of companies, making it just as necessary to shop around comparing the different deals on offer. If you choose a camping safari in this way, ask the agency the same questions you would ask the operators themselves. Too many agents stay behind their desks in Nairobi seldom venturing out to check on the actualities of the safaris they recommend.

Let's Go Travel, Caxton House, Standard Street (near the GPO) offer an efficient booking service popular with tourists and residents and represent a wide range of companies with camping safaris to suit all budgets and time limits. If you want to go it alone, Let's Go have their own fleet of hire cars and rent Camping Boxes containing tent, stove and other essential items needed for independent camping safaris. Let's Go also deal with internal and international air flights, lodge and hotel bookings, and produce a series of information leaflets for visitors to Kenya. For details telephone 29539, 29540, 340331.

If contacting any of these companies in advance, from within or from outside Kenya, the PO Box number must be included in the address.

PUBLIC TRANSPORT

Matatus run on set routes around cities and towns, or between towns and outlying villages. These generally keep to no set timetable, and leave when they are full.

Buses operate long distance between main towns, and often cover the same local routes as matatus. Buses tend to be slightly cheaper and less frequent, but slower (and therefore safer).

When searching for road transport, ask around in the market or bus/matatu station for a vehicle heading in your direction. If there is a choice take the one with the most people aboard as that will leave first.

Kenya's train service is fairly reliable and is a viable alternative to road transport over long distances, although some of the lines shown on maps run irregular services or no longer operate at all. Trains run between Nairobi and Kisumu or Malaba on the Kenya/Uganda border, between Konza and Magadi in the south, and between Voi and Taveta south of Tsavo West National Park. The train journey between Nairobi and Mombasa can cut out a long drive or bus ride, and is a tourist attraction in its own right.

Kenya Airways operates a number of internal air services between Nairobi, Mombasa and some other large towns or tourist areas. Private air companies also operate a limited number of flights. If time is short, or if you want to avoid a long stretch of driving, or quite simply want to fly for the sheer pleasure of it, contact Let's Go Travel (mentioned on the previous page), or another travel agent, for full details.

HITCH-HIKING

Hitch-hiking in Kenya is only for those with plenty of time and patience, but it is a cheap, safe, and interesting way to travel. On some routes lifts are easy to find, while on others you may have to spend all day at the side of the road. But this is no problem for campers; if you get stuck late at night, and conditions allow, put up the tent and start again in the morning.

On main roads, and in more populated areas, you shouldn't have to wait too long. People in private cars will probably give you a free lift, although lorry drivers may expect payment. The price should normally be less than the bus fare over the same route, and you are unlikely to be overcharged. Do not use the usual hitchers' thumb sign when hitching as this may be misinterpreted in a number of ways. Wave your hand up and down or in the direction you want to go. A hand held high means you want to go a long way, held low means you are only going locally.

With patience and luck, and probably with a bit of walking in between, you can reach many out-of-the-way places. We have met intrepid hitchers who have hitched along the Mau Escarpment, halfway up Mount Kenya, and all the way around Lake Naivasha. Others have reached Loyangalani from Maralal and Moyale from Marsabit, and two hitchers we met had even made it up to Ileret, just about as far north as you can go.

The biggest problem for hitchers is getting into national parks, as only visitors in vehicles are allowed in, but even here you may get lucky at the gate and find somebody willing to fit you into their car.

There are advantages and disadvantages to all the forms of transport described above. Taking an organised camping safari means no planning headaches; you choose your safari, pick a date, pay your money, and everything else is taken care of. On an organised safari, though, you can become somewhat removed from Kenyan day-to-day life, never meeting the people or really getting to know the places you pass through.

This aspect of isolation or insularity can also be a disadvantage when camping with a car, although in your own vehicle you get more freedom and flexibility, stopping when and where you like, with no set itineraries to keep. Mechanical know-how is an obvious advantage if you plan to leave the main routes, and security is also a point to consider, especially if you plan to leave the vehicle while walking and camping in a mountain area. (For more details see the *Security* section.)

Hitching and public transport can be slower than travelling with your own car, but you still get some choice of route and destination without any of the mechanical or security worries involved with taking your own vehicle.

You will probably find that a combination of all forms of transport and travelling in Kenya will be the most convenient and the most interesting.

WALKING AND CYCLING

Kenya has many escarpments, ranges of hills, and mountain massifs that make ideal walking and backpacking country. This is where the independent traveller with a tent really has an advantage. Some campsites covered in this book can only be reached by walkers, and are fully described in the relevant sections.

With a bike and a tent, once again, you can go anywhere in Kenya. Traditional touring machines will cope on most tar and dirt roads without any trouble. Kenyan motorists are more cause for alarm than any road surface. Make sure you know what is coming up behind you, and be prepared to take evasive action onto the verge, as many Kenyan cyclists are often forced to do. A mirror is worth considering, and cruising with a Walkman on is just asking for trouble.

Carrying bikes on buses is no problem, and useful if long uninteresting sections need to be crossed, although lightweight machines can sometimes be damaged if not loaded carefully.

For more serious off-roaders an ATB, or mountain bike, is recommended. It may be possible to hire one from Gametrackers (see page 15). You can explore the Cherangani Mountains or the lakeside roads south-west of Kisumu, or at Hell's Gate, near Lake Naivasha, you can pitch your tent and ride through a national park, past herds of zebra and gazelle, with baboons in the bushes at the roadside.

Chapter 5

Equipment and Provisions

The equipment that you take for camping in Kenya depends very much on how you intend to travel. With a car you can carry more, and the vehicle itself generates its own load as spare parts, jerry cans and sand ramps have to be added. At the other end of the scale, if you are hitching, everything has to be fitted into a rucksack and you are limited to what you can carry practicably on your back.

Whichever way you travel, always take things because you need them, not simply because there is space. An overloaded vehicle is harder to drive and more liable to damage. A heavy rucksack is cumbersome on buses, makes you vulnerable on city streets, and limits your backpacking range in the hills.

Large canvas safari tents, camping chairs and tables, *pangas*, spades, and other heavy duty gear are available at a number of specialist stores on Muindi Mbingu Street and Biashara Street in Nairobi, but light-weight camping equipment is not readily available in Kenya. A few shops supply tents, sleeping bags and stoves but the quality is usually poor or the goods highly expensive.

Lightweight camping and backpacking gear is available in any good outdoor equipment shop, and should be bought before leaving for Kenya. For specialist safari equipment SafariQuip, 13a Waterloo Park, Upper Brook Street, Stockport SK1 3BP, Tel: (061) 429 8700, have a comprehensive mail order service.

It is better to bring all the specialist equipment that you will require, but if you really need something in Nairobi try Adam Ltd on Muindi Mbingu Street, who sell gaz stoves for 650/−, disposable refills for 35/−, sleeping bags for around 1000/−, and tents for around 2000/−. Atul's Ltd on Biashara Street sell secondhand tents for around 1500/−, and sleeping bags for between 450/− and 1500/−. Atul's also rent equipment including tents 75/− per day, roof-racks 50/− per day, cool boxes 50/− per day, and walking boots 40/− per day.

It is often possible to buy secondhand tents and equipment from other travellers. Check the notice boards at Mrs Roche's, the youth hostel, or in the popular budget hotels.

TENTS

A tent is obviously your most important item, and probably the most difficult to choose. A very wide range of styles, designs, and materials are available.

If you are carrying all your gear in a rucksack then lightness and compactness is a major consideration. With a car, lightness is not so important; you can afford a bit more space and weight. Large canvas tents with wooden poles or metal frames are roomy but very heavy and generally only used by up-market safari companies. Aluminium frame tents are lighter and ideal for family holidays, but are seldom found in Kenya. Frame tents are generally stable and can be pitched on any ground, but they are often bulky to carry and cannot withstand strong winds.

So practicalities dictate that most car campers use the same style of lightweight nylon tents favoured by backpackers. And if you plan to travel in Kenya using a variety of forms of transport then this type of tent will be ideal however you go.

Style

Many backpackers' tents are still based on the tried and tested design involving two upright poles at either end of the tent joined by a horizontal ridge pole. Variations on this design include: sloping ridge poles, making the tent smaller and more streamlined against the wind; A-frames, for more stability and easier access; wedge-shaped tents with twin parallel poles at the front, which give more headroom and even easier access, but can be unstable in high winds.

More modern designs include parallel hooped 'tunnel' tents which rely on sets of thin tensioned poles. An improvement on this design involves cross-hooped 'dome' tents which are more stable in windy conditions and flap less. Both tunnel and dome tents tend to have more headroom than ridge tents, although they can be comparatively heavy.

A free-standing tent, not relying totally on pegs and guys, is useful on rocky or sandy ground, or in thick grass. In Kenya you are likely to be camping on this type of ground quite often!

Most tents are double skin, with an inner tent covered by a separate fly sheet, and this design is usually prefered by backpackers. An inner tent made of cotton can 'breathe' and is less prone to condensation, while nylon is lighter to carry, especially if wet. Some single skin tents are available made of breathable fabric, but the performance of such tents is impaired if they are well ventilated, making them unsuitable for warm and wet conditions.

Space
In the endless search for weight saving improvements, some tents are very small and allow little room for movement. Undressing in such a tent requires contortionist's skills, even getting into your sleeping bag can be a delicate move, and cooking inside the tent is completely out of the question. So, bearing this in mind, take the smallest and lightest tent that will be comfortable. If you plan to travel for a long period, a little extra space inside the tent will soon be appreciated.

If you are tall check that there is enough space to stretch out at night. Touching the tent walls will cause distortion and leaking during rain. In some backpacking tents you sleep across the tent with your feet and head in the angle of the canvas. Even for people of average height this can be uncomfortable.

Assembly
A tent should be quick and easy to put up. You do not want to spend a long while pegging out flysheets or assembling poles if it is getting cold and dark halfway up Mount Kenya, or the afternoon rainstorm is just about to break. A tent where the flysheet goes up before the inner is also useful in the rain, but if the whole thing goes up quickly anyway this is not of the utmost importance.

Facilities
A sewn-in groundsheet keeps out water and insects. Adequate fixings for guy ropes and fly sheet are also necessary to combat wind and rain on mountains or on the coast.

Mosquito netting is absolutely essential. If you already have a tent with no insect protection adapt it with netting and glue or velcro. To camp without netting means you will have to be so tightly zipped up you will sweat buckets or suffocate, or alternatively risk opening the door and get bitten all over instead.

For camping in hot areas a tent with two openings allows a cooling draught to blow through. Two doors means you can cook in one entrance while using the other door for coming in and out.

Other points to check
When buying a tent check the quality of the stitching; seams under strain should be double stitched. Check also that zips and peg loops are firmly attached, and that seams are sealed against rain. Amazingly, some manufacturers sell tents with unsealed seams. If necessary seal or re-seal the seams on your tent. Seam-sealant is available in equipment stores. (Not in Kenya.)

Mount Elgon crater.

For ridge or wedge tents, check how the poles are joined together. Are the springs strong? If the poles are designed to fit inside one another can they be easily separated? On hooped tents, how are the poles attached to the canvas? Wider sleeves means the poles are easier to insert and less likely to chafe the tent walls when erected.

If possible carry a small length of aluminium tube to act as a sleeve to repair a broken pole. Another good idea is to sew a ring onto your tent at the bottom of the zip to allow it to be secured with a small padlock.

We used a Wild Country Quasar when we were in Kenya, and although it was slightly too big and heavy for the times when we were lightweight backpacking, for general travelling it was ideal. It stood up to sub-zero temperatures on Mount Elgon, and withstood violent monsoons at Malindi. It protected us against mosquitoes in Kakamega Forest and against dust storms at Lake Turkana. A free-standing dome tent of this type can be highly recommended. We heard a few traveller's tales about these tents, though:

One camper in a large brown dome tent claimed to have spent an evening chasing off amorous hippos who mistook the tent for a potential mate. Another traveller told us about an elephant attracted to a campsite by the smell of fresh fruit eaten earlier by a camper sleeping inside one of the tents. Unable to reach the fruit the elephant picked up the whole tent, with the fruit and the camper (by this time wide awake) held inside by the sewn-in groundsheet. After a few half-hearted swings of the tent the elephant was chased off, and the camper lived to eat fruit another day. Although probably never again inside his tent!

SLEEPING EQUIPMENT

Sleeping bag

Because of the wide range of climatic conditions found in Kenya, from searing desert in the north to permanent snow on Mount Kenya, a sleeping bag has to be fairly versatile. A 2− or 3−season bag should be sufficient for all but the very coldest conditions. A bag fitted with a zip allows some flexibility; you can open the bag to get a cooling breeze or zip right up against the cold. A zip conducts the cold so should have padding behind it.

Down bags are warm and compact but compress easily under your body. Holofil, and more recently Qualofil, bags are not so compact, but hold their warmth retaining bulk and only lose a little of their efficiency when wet. They are also cheaper.

We have found that two lightweight 2−season bags used together make an excellent combination. On warm nights only one bag is used and the other becomes a mattress. In cold conditions both bags are used and seem more effective than a single bag of the same weight and bulk. This 'system' concept is not new, but some manufacturers are now selling sets of sleeping bags designed to be used in this way.

A sheet sleeping bag provides another layer on cold nights, and is useful on its own when the weather is warm. It also stops the inside of your sleeping bag from becoming too dirty.

Silver reflective 'space blankets' are very light and good in an emergency, but they do not allow any body moisture to escape which can freeze in extremely cold conditions.

Mosquito net

Many travellers carry separate mosquito nets for the occasions when they may be sleeping in hotels or lodges where nets are not supplied. In a large frame tent, a net that hangs from a single point and covers the bed or sleeping mat, is useful. In smaller tents where all the doors and vents are covered in good netting, separate nets are not necessary.

If you do not have a mosquito net then pitch your tent on the bed in your hotel room. This will also protect you from bed-bugs!

Camp bed, Sleeping mat

Beds and mats cut down on the bumps and provide a layer of insulation between your body and the ground. In large tents there may be room for traditional style canvas camp beds with metal frames that are easily dismantled, although the metal legs can damage groundsheets.

Backpackers, however, will not have room for such luxuries and will have to rely on closed cell foam mats, or Karrimats, which are light and effective but can be bulky. This is no problem in a car, but to save space if you are backpacking, they can be trimmed down to about half size. Put the mat under your body between shoulders and hips, use a jacket or sweatshirt as a pillow and rest your legs on your empty rucksack.

Other options include inflatable Lilos, and self-inflating Calipaks or ThermaRests.

COOKING EQUIPMENT

When camping in Kenya, open wood fires have a traditional and evocative appeal, but it is more practical to remember that firewood is not always available, and rain makes a fire difficult to light. If you plan to leave the main routes for a while, cooked food or a hot cup of tea is something you cannot do without, so for all campers a stove is highly recommended.

Backpackers can provide for themselves with a single compact stove, while campers with vehicles can afford the luxury of two stoves and prepare more adventurous meals when on safari.

Four main types of stove are available: paraffin (kerosene), methylated spirits (meths), liquid gas, and petrol (gasoline).

Paraffin/Kerosene, (called Kerosene in Kenya), is readily available as many local people use it for their own stoves. It is safer than petrol, but oily and messy. Paraffin stoves need meths or paste for priming and require frequent pumping to maintain pressure.

Meths stoves are very simple, light to carry, and easy to operate, although they burn fuel faster than petrol stoves and cannot produce the same level of heat. The meths stoves most favoured by campers are made by Trangia, not usually available in Kenya. Although meths is not as widely available as petrol in Kenya, it can often be found in chemists or hardware shops. Chemists charge more, but hardware shops may dilute the meths. Expect to pay around 25/– for 750 ml.

Liquid gas stoves usually use butane, or a butane/propane mix for

extemely cold or high altitude conditions. The small sizes of cartridge are generally disposable, while the larger cylinders are refillable. Small Camping Gaz butane cartridges (size C206) are available for around 35/−, and large cylinders (sizes 904 and 907) can be bought and re-filled in Nairobi. In other parts of Kenya, however, replacements and refills are hard to find. Note also that gas canisters or cylinders cannot be carried on aeroplanes.

Some makes of petrol stoves only run on lead-free petrol (white gas) which is not available in Kenya. Others run on low grade fuel which is readily and cheaply found in most populated regions for around 10/− per litre. Leaded petrol can cause stoves to clog. Self priming stoves require pumping to build up pressure, while other require priming with meths before lighting. Petrol stoves loose efficiency when used on cold ground. We used a small Optimus petrol stove for all our travels in Kenya, and it never let us down.

Various makes of stoves are available that can be quickly and easily adapted to run on different types of fuel. A good outdoor equipment shop will be able to advise you further.

Metal bottles with tight screw-top lids are best for carrying fuel. Litre bottles are handy; never try to fill a stove from a 50 litre jerry can. Other useful items include: a windshield, a stiff sheet of cardboard or aluminium will do; a pricker to clear the jets on petrol or paraffin stoves which are not self-pricking. When buying your stove check which parts are likely to need replacing. Small spare parts are not available in Kenya.

When conditions allow − in dry, well-wooded areas − an open fire can be used. Use stones to support your cooking pots. A 'backpacker's grill' (just a piece of wire mesh) can be very useful for grilling fish or meat over a fire. Car campers can carry a grid-iron to rest on stones and a 'debbie' (a big tin can on legs) to heat water. Rubbing soap on the outside of the pots before they go on the fire makes them easy to clean. Open fires can be energy and time consuming, but do save fuel, and relaxing next to a blazing camp fire with a coffee after your meal is a lot more pleasant than huddling around a gas burner or petrol stove! More importantly an open fire will keep animals at a respectful distance.

Backpackers will need to carry a mess tin, or a compact set of billies (cooking pots). Some makes of stoves come complete with one or two integral nesting pots. Lids conserve heat, reduce cooking time, and double as plates if necessary. A wooden spoon, a sharp knife, a plastic or enamel plate, bowl and cup, and a set of cutlery is all you need to be completely self-contained.

For car campers, space and weight are not so vital, so luxuries such as kettles and frying pans can be included, but do not fall into the trap of carrying too much unnecessary equipment.

Aluminium pots in various sizes, wooden spoons, plastic cups and bowls, and cutlery, all ideal for camping safaris, are readily and cheaply available in markets and *dukas* all over Kenya.

WATER PURIFICATION

For campers in Kenya one of the most important factors to consider is the supply of water. Clean water is essential if you are going to enjoy your safari. Various organisms exist in contaminated water which can lead to an upset stomach or even a serious disease.

In Nairobi the water from the taps is usually safe to drink although in smaller towns the chlorine supply may not be so reliable. Even in the wilds stream or well water may be polluted by human or animal waste.

For cooking, water that has been boiled vigorously is usually safe, but remember that water boils at a lower temperature at high altitude, so may not destroy all the organisms.

For drinking while backpacking (and you need to drink more in hot climates) it may not be possible or convenient to boil water. If you can, use a filter to clear the water of debris and large organisms. Specialised filters are available for this purpose, but a fine piece of cloth is better than nothing. For the smaller organisms use a water purification agent. Chlorine-based tablets are effective but taste unpleasant. Silver based tablets or solutions leave no taste but may not be completely safe against all protozoa and should be used with a filter.

Car-campers have a whole range of heavy duty filters to chose from. Most are available from SafariQuip (address p. 21). For backpackers, and all travellers trying to keep their weight down, a Travel Well may be suitable. This new gadget uses a unique treatment method to purify even the most contaminated water. A military version of the Travel Well is also available which fits directly onto a water bottle. More information from Pre-mac (Kent) Ltd, Unit 1, 103 Goods Station Rd, Tunbridge Wells, Kent TN1 2DP, Tel: (0892) 34361, or from MASTA.

Just beacuse you may be roughing it a bit on safari, it doesn't mean your diet has to suffer. With a bit of thought you can cook quite elaborate meals. If you pitch camp early, preparing the food is all part of the fun, not a chore to be quicky completed. With help from some of the plastic sachets of brandy that are available in many Kenyan bars, we managed to produce flambée bananas in the middle of the Chalbi Desert. (Elizabeth Slinn, Nairobi)

SAFARI LISTS

Below are two lists of camping equipment. The first is supplied by Ben Rode and Nancy O'Donnel (USA), two very experienced campers who, during the time they have lived and worked in Kenya, have travelled very widely to various parts of the country. Their list is the result of many safaris, and many forgotten items. They do not always take everything on the list, but it serves as a useful reminder for them, as it will for anyone planning a car safari.

We found Ben and Nancy's list very useful when we were camping with a car. At the other end of the scale is our own backpacking list. To save as much weight as possible, we have reduced everything to a bare minimum. This list is the result of many foot safaris, and many discarded items!

Ben and Nancy's list

Tent
Hammer
Shovel
Panga, shears
Saw, axe
Work gloves
Car tools and spares
Rope
Sleeping mats
Sleeping bags
Pillows
Table
Chairs
Jerry can (petrol)
Water carriers
Grid iron/Grill
Debbie
Kitchen knife
Bread knife
Skewers
Potato peeler
Wooden spoon
Spatula
Barbeque fork
Can opener
Bottle opener
Strainer
Oven gloves
Plates, bowls
Cups, mugs
Knives, forks, spoons
Wine glasses

Matches
Torch/Flashlight
Batteries
Gas lamp
Gas stove
Cooking fuel
Funnel
Tarpaulin
Wellington boots
Umbrella
Thermos flask
Saucepans
Frying pan
Kettle
Coffee pot
Tin foil
Cutting board
Wash cloth/sponge
Pot scrubber
Tea towels
Clothes line, pegs
Binoculars
Camera, films
Bird, animal books
Maps
Towels
Toothbrush, paste
Flannel/Face cloth
Soap, shampoo
Tick powder
First Aid kit (see below)
Sun block

Washing up bowl	Sun glasses
Drainer	Clothes
Washing up liquid	Money, papers

All this equipment fits into a Suzuki SJ.

Dave and Jill's backpacking list

Tent	First Aid kit
Sleeping bags, sheet inners	Sewing kit
Sleeping mats	1 small towel
Stove	1 flannel/face cloth
750 ml fuel bottle	Soap, shampoo
1 litre water bottle	Toothbrush, paste
Collapsable water carrier	Washing soap
2 cooking pots	Maps
2 plates, mugs	Cameras, film
1 fork, 1 spoon	Sunglasses
Sharp knife	Sun cream
Swiss Army Knife	Clothes

This was carried between two people in two 55 litre packs weighing about 12 kg each.

First Aid Kit

Backpackers are not able to carry too much and should stick to the basics. This is what we carry when we are hiking and travelling by car:

sticking plasters/Band Aids	aspirin/paracetamol
antiseptic powder and cream	powerful pain killers
anti-diarrhoea tablets	oil of cloves (for toothache)
lip protector stick	malaria pills
mosquito repellent	water purifiers
antihistamine cream	safety pins.
intensive care cream (for dry or cracked skin)	

It is not necessary to carry large supplies of basic items, as they can be replaced from pharmacies in Nairobi and large towns.

Other items also carried by travellers in Kenya include:

bandages and tubigrips	disposable syringes
travel sickness pills	antibiotics

Broad spectrum antibiotics can be used for treating a wide range of bacterial infections (external or internal) but, unless you are familiar with medicines, it is not recommended that you prescribe these drugs to yourself. Get good advice about what types of antibiotics to carry and when to use them. Incorrect or 'casual' use of antibiotics can be dangerous or lessen their effectiveness.

More information is available in the travellers' health books described in *Suggested Reading*.

RUCKSACKS

Rucksacks, or backpacks, are of obvious use to hitchers and campers without their own vehicle, but even if you are travelling with a car, a rucksack is highly recommended. Suitcases are impractical and liable to damage, while rucksacks are pliable and pack easily, and are much more useful if you plan to leave the car to hike on mountains or around lakes. If you are unlikely to leave your vehicle then a tough kitbag is a good idea.

If you are travelling by public transport, or expect to hitch, make sure your pack is strong enough to stand up to long rough rides on a bus roof-rack or lorry. External frame rucksacks are cumbersome and easily damaged. An internal frame pack is far more comfortable and convenient.

When buying a rucksack, get the best you can afford. Chose one made with strong material, and check the seams, zips, buckles and straps. A cheaply made rucksack using components of inferior quality may let you down in the wilds and good quality bags are not usually available in Kenya.

Large companies manufacturing rucksacks and outdoor equipment usually offer a very wide selection of packs readily available at numerous outlets, and base their product designs on years of experience and widespread customer feedback with additional advice from specialist consultants. Smaller companies, while not having the wide range, often produce packs which are well made, and more reasonably priced.

CLOTHES

Campers travelling widely in Kenya are likely to experience a wide range of climates. Clothes should therefore be as adaptable and as versatile as possible. The following list of basics will be about the same for backpackers and car campers: 2 pairs of long trousers or one pair of long trousers and a skirt, one pair of shorts, two long sleeved shirts, one or two tee-shirts, one sweatshirt, two or three pairs of socks, three or four sets of underwear, one pair of strong shoes or boots, one pair of sandals, one jacket, one hat.

Trousers and shirts should be loose fitting, and made of heavy cotton, or cotton mix, or one of the durable lightweight fabrics made by specialist outdoor manufacturers. Clothes made from natural materials tend to be less compact in your pack. Specialist synthetics can get sweaty and uncomfortable when driving or sitting on a bus for a long time. Denim is tough but hard to wash and not suitable for walking as it gets very heavy when wet.

Shoes are a personal matter. For backpackers trying to keep weight down, one pair for everything is preferable. We have always found good training shoes (running shoes) suitable for most uses. Other campers prefer boots to shoes, or may find leather more comfortable.

A jacket is especially useful in the rainy season, and also necessary if you are in the mountains. It should be windproof, waterproof, and easy to pack. There will be many times when the jacket is not needed, so it should not take up too much space in your pack. Breathable fabrics have many advantages.

A hat which keeps sun and rain off is recommended for travel in Kenya. An army type bush hat is ideal.

A thermal vest is an optional extra. They are light to carry and very warm next to the skin in cold conditions.

Remember to make the most of your clothes. Take clothes that can be worn comfortably together as layers if necessary.

Locally made safari outfits are available in a number of shops in Nairobi, but if you want to obtain specialist safari clothing and accessories before you leave, Travelling Light have a comprehensive mail order catalogue. In the UK phone (09314) 488 for details.

Chapter 6

Miscellaneous Information

NATIONAL PARKS AND RESERVES

Kenya's national parks and reserves were originally called game parks. Hunting is now strictly controlled and although the wild animals can no longer be regarded as game, the term 'game park' still exists as a convenient catch-all phrase. National parks are controlled by the central National Parks Department, part of the Ministry of Tourism and Wildlife. National reserves are controlled locally by individual district councils. Both parks and reserves have public campsites and special campsites.

Public campsites can be used by any person visiting the park on payment of the nightly camping fee. This is normally payable at your entry gate. Pay in advance for the number of nights you intend to stay in the park. Some public sites have permanent guards or are visited by park staff to check camping fees have been paid. If you decide to stay longer in the park, you should return to a gate to pay the extra or pay the amount you owe when you leave.

Special Campsites can be reserved for the exclusive use of any person or group for one week. The special campsite reservation fee is usually 1000/- (300/- in some parks) per site per week (psw). The site can be reserved in advance by writing to the warden (allow 2 − 6 weeks for a reply), or if the site is unoccupied it can be reserved on arrival. Payment is made on arrival in both cases and the nightly camping fee must also be paid. Special campsites are generally in remote areas of the parks and have no facilities; consequently some special sites are seldom used. Special campsites were originally established for hunters and in some parks are still called professional campsites.

Entrance fees also have to be paid at national parks and reserves. These are paid at your entry gate but are only paid once, irrespective of the number of days you intend to stay. Camping fees are paid per person per night (ppn).

National Park Entrance Fees

	Non-Resident	Resident/Citizen
Adult	80/-	15/-
Child	5/-	2/-
Student	20/-	5/-
Car	30/-	15/-
Minibus	50/-	25/-
Camping	30/-	10/-

Note: It is proposed (1990) to raise fees to US$10.

National reserve entrance fees are similar although non-resident adults pay 50/−. Entrance fees are generally standardised across the country, although there are some slight discrepancies between different parks and reserves. Students (including school children) are only given discount when in organised groups; ISIC cards are not usually accepted. The status of temporary residents can vary. Some parks and reserves also make a nightly charge for campers' vehicles.

Parks and reserves generally open at 0600 h. Last entry is 1815 h and the gates close at 1900 h.

A vehicle is required to enter virtually all the national parks and reserves in Kenya. Walkers are permitted to walk in some parks, only in professionally organised groups with prior arrangement with the warden. Hitching into parks, for those with tact, patience and luck, is possible but very difficult. Public transport and hitching information is given in the relevant sections of this book.

Various maps of national parks and reserves are available which are generally reliable. Because of the very nature of national parks however, maps cannot show every single track and so some confusion may arise. In many parks junctions are numbered to help map reading, or main features of the park are signposted. At entrance gates distances to lodges, campsites, and other gates are often displayed.

Two wheel drive (2WD) vehicles can enter most parks and visit certain areas without difficulty in the dry season. To reach remote areas, or during the wet season, four wheel drive (4WD) and high clearance is necessary.

Drive slowly in the parks. You are much more likely to see animals, and less likely to damage the park by throwing up dust. 20 kph is recommended. Leaving official roads and tracks is forbidden in most parks as you may get lost, stuck or run out of petrol. More importantly, most parks exist in a precarious environmental balance and vehicles leaving the tracks cause considerable erosion.

In the wet season, or just afterwards, the parks are at their finest scenically, but animals may be harder to spot. In the dry season the grass is lower and animals tend to congregate at rivers or water-holes. Game is often attracted to lodges by artificial water-holes and baits. This is a good place to see the animals, but these viewing sites tend to be popular. In the well-known parks at high season the number of tourist vehicles can be very high. This spoils much of the experience for many visitors, and on a more practical level can make photos of animals difficult to capture without a safari minibus or two in the background. Only by limiting the number of vehicles permitted in each park, can this situation be avoided.

In some parks and reserves it is permitted to leave your vehicle at certain points. When walking in parks remember the constant presence of wild animals; you are not in a zoo. Do not walk stealthily. Be as noisy as possible to warn animals of your presence. Once aware, most animals will prefer to leave you alone and you will see nothing more than footprints and a pile of fresh droppings. A surprised or cornered animal is a potentially dangerous animal. The same applies when setting up camp in remote or little used campsites. Pitch noisily and light a fire. This way you may get a few animals passing by to have a look, but you will not surprise any into attack.

At popular sites most animals will stay clear of humans, although in some parks the animals have become so used to people they are no longer afraid and come to the sites at night to scavenge. Baboons are a particular problem. Never attempt to feed animals, and never leave food around.

Although not officially permitted, with the rangers' permission, it is often possible to camp near a park gate (ie those without campsites) if you arrive after the park gate has closed.

Wherever you camp in the national parks and reserves, or if you are camping wild in other remote parts of Kenya, try to do as little damage as possible. Bury deeply all toilet waste if no toilet is provided. Burn all rubbish properly and bury the remains. Never bury cans; animals will dig them up. All litter that will not burn completely should be taken away. Even biodegradable waste is undesirable as any litter encourages others to drop more. Take a strong plastic bag or cardboard box to use as a litter bin.

Some campsites without facilities are being spoilt by inconsiderate campers going to the toilet behind bushes and trees very close to where tents are pitched. Campers should always move far away from the campsite and preferably bury their mess. I always take some matches with me, and burn the toilet paper I've used there and then. (Debbie Clarke, Australia)

THE COAST

Most of the campsites on the coast are privately owned and run, so prices and conditions vary considerably. Like the country club and hotel campsites inland, the bungalow sites on the coast which allow camping usually have a good range of facilities including bar, restaurant and even swimming pools, and so are ideal for families, or lazy campers!

In April and May the winds blow onshore, carrying seaweed and other debris on to the beaches. During the rest of the year the beaches are generally clean, and the water is clear, especially away from Mombasa and other large towns.

A coral reef runs parallel to the coastline along much of its length, which is possible to reach in some places by walking across the coral platform at low tide. Plastic shoes should be worn to protect the feet from coral and various spiky sea creatures.

A number of Marine National Parks have been established along the coast, giving fish, plants and coral the same protection enjoyed by mammals in the parks and reserves elsewhere in Kenya. The Kenyan government must be applauded for creating these marine parks. So go snorkelling and enjoy the multi-coloured underwater paradise, but if you break off any coral not only is it illegal and pointless because the colours fade when the coral dries, but you are deliberately destroying a living thing. You would not pull a gazelle's horns off in Amboseli, so do not break off bits of coral in Malindi Reef either.

Even outside marine national parks sea life should be protected. Do not buy coral or shells from salesmen. This encourages them to break coral or poach living molluscs to sell to insensitive tourists.

Silversands campsite, Malindi.

HEALTH

When travelling in Kenya (or any Third World country) the different climatic and social conditions means visitors are exposed to diseases that are not normally found at home. Campers experience this exposure just as much as any other tourist, but due to the independence that most campers enjoy they can actually do more than most about prevention.

Although you will have received all the recommended vaccinations before arriving in Kenya, remember that you are not completely invulnerable, and certain precautions still have to be taken.

Read a good travel medical book (see *Suggested Reading*) and be aware of the causes, symptoms and treatments of the more serious diseases. Do not let colourful descriptions put you off though. With common sense and a little care most of the illnesses can be avoided.

Many diseases (including dysentery, cholera, giardia and infective hepatitis) are transmitted through unclean food and water. Infected plates, cups and cutlery can also be a cause. Thus, although it is sometimes harder when camping to maintain high standards of hygiene, if you do keep your eating equipment clean, thoroughly cook your own food, boil your own drinking water, and wash your hands well before preparing or eating food, you probably stand less chance of contracting any kind of food or water transmitted disease than tourists staying in hotels and lodges.

Other diseases which are of particular relevance include bilharzia or schistosomiasis which is carried by small parasitic worms that enter your body through drinking or swimming in infected water. Trypanosomiasis, or sleeping sickness, is carried by the tsetse fly and transmitted to humans by the fly's bite.

Campers are also exposed to malaria, but like all diseases, the chances of contracting this disease can be reduced if the appropriate preventitive steps are taken. Malaria is caused by a blood parasite which is transmitted to humans via the bite of an infected mosquito. No vaccine is currently available, so a course of pills has to be taken. In some parts of Kenya it has been reported that certain species of malaria parasite have developed resistance to particular types of anti-malarial drug. If your doctor is not familiar with current conditions, contact one of the medical advice centres listed in *Preparations*.

Pills do not provide total protection so other precautions are necessary. Wear long sleeved shirts and long trousers in the evening, as mosquitoes are only usually found at this time, especially if you are pitched in long grass or near water, and zip up the netting and doors on your tent in good time. Some travellers carry anti-mosquito spray which can be useful. This can be bought in Nairobi.

Avoid spreading diseases yourself by acting responsibly and following the directions about disposing of waste in the *National Parks* section above.

SECURITY

At the campsites in national parks and reserves robbery is unlikely; monkeys and baboons are likely to be more of a problem than human thieves, and in areas where there is a risk sites are usually well guarded or lit up at night. Many campsites, as a matter of course, have a guard at night (*askari*). (Wherever possible, the security situation is described with the individual campsite details).

With organised camping safaris the cook, or another member of staff, stays with the tents all the time and there is no risk.

Obviously, when camping wild, the further away from human habitation you pitch your tent the more unlikely you are to be disturbed, although in remote towns or isolated settlements unused to tourists, theft of any kind is almost unheard of. Securing your tent with a small padlock will deter inquisitive children and animals.

In Nairobi, however, and at popular resorts on the coast, theft from tourists is a growing problem. New arrivals are the easiest targets, so be at your most alert in the first few days. Beware of pick-pockets on buses and in crowded places. Avoid walking in City Park, Uhuru Park, and the area around the museum at night.

A number of con-men operate in Nairobi pretending to be students or Ugandan refugees looking for sponsorship. Others offer to change money. Ignore them all.

New arrivals in Nairobi stick out like a sore thumb. You can imagine a con-man's delight when he sees a fresh, pale-skinned tourist walking around town with a huge rucksack on, or with their nose stuck in the map section of a guide book. After a few days, when things get familiar, it's easier to give an impression that you know what you're doing and the number of con-men who do approach you falls rapidly.

When I first arrived in Nairobi, I was struck by the friendliness of all the people. Many wanted to know where I was from, when I had arrived, and what I thought of Kenya. It took several conversations for me to to realise that they were all asking the same questions and telling similar stories. Many said they were refugees from Uganda, coming to Kenya to look for places to study at. On one occasion I was invited to join a group in a small cafe, where they reeled off an impressive list of British universities and asked my advice on each of them. Then they came to their main problem; they needed money. Would I be able to lend them some money for fees, then they would repay me when they graduated…?

At this point we were approached by two more characters who asked to have a private word with me. They produced police identification, and told me the 'friends' I had been with, who had quietly slipped away, were known con-men currently on probation. As I started to leave the policemen started asking me the same old questions: Where was I from? How long had I been in Kenya? And then they started telling me how generous other tourists had been after they'd been saved from the clutches of the con-men. Would I like to help them…?

And this was just the first day! (Matthew Rowntree, Britain)

Animal Dangers

For campers a tent forms an effective barrier between you and the wildlife, with only occasional incidents of animals entering tents. At the bottom of most stories the cause is usually human carelessness rather than aggressive animals. Never keep food inside your tent unless in an unopened can. The slightest smell may attract inquisitive animals.

Usually though, with sufficient warning, animals will try to avoid human contact. Follow the directions given in the *National Parks and Reserves* section when walking in areas where there is likely to be game. Never try to creep up on animals on foot unless you are with an experienced guide or ranger.

Although lions can be dangerous, contrary to Hollywood myth, crocodile and buffalo cause most fatalities in Kenya. Two rules which are not myths, and well worth obeying are never get between a mother elephant and her young or between a hippo and the water. Even if you are in a car.

Snakes are rarely seen and are seldom a cause for campers' concern. Most of Kenya's snakes are harmless anyway, but like all animals they try to avoid human contact and vanish at the sound of footsteps. The biggest risk comes from the puff adder which relys on camouflage in long grass as its defence and may not always move away when disturbed.

The most dangerous of all Kenya's animals is the mosquito which carries malaria. For more details see the *Health* section.

NATURAL HISTORY

Many tourists visit Kenya to see 'The Big Five' large game animals, and other popular, easily recognisable, favourites, but there are plenty of other animals to look out for, and a great many birds to spot. Viewing the more obscure species of Kenya's wildlife is interesting and very enjoyable once you have aquired some basic knowlege. A field guide and set of binoculars are invaluable for sorting out gazelle and impala, or identifying birds perched on distant treetops.

Animals

Kenya's geography and biology is very varied and contains representative sections of coastal woodland, moorland plains, semi-desert scrub, high altitude rain forest, and all their associated wildlife, making the whole country an ideal place to see most of the zoological species of Africa. In addition Kenya has some unique animals ranging from the tiny duiker in the Arabuko-Sokoke forest on the coast to the salt mining elephants in the caves of Mount Elgon.

The continued survival of many species is being severely limited by man's colonisation; the human population of Kenya is growing at an alarming rate. National parks and reserves endeavour to preserve examples of all habitats and the wildlife they support. Particularly vulnerable species, eg rhinos and elephants are the subject of special conservation measures including translocation and continuous surveillance. Nevertheless poachers still manage to operate with virtual impunity and threaten to completely destroy Kenya's entire rhinoceros population.

Some of the parks themselves, by their very nature, have added to the problem. When large animals such as elephants cannot leave the protected areas, either because of the damage they cause in neighbouring farmland or due to the fickle demands of tourism, the land has no time to recover from their browsing and becomes severely eroded. When the trees and bushes, and finally the topsoil, have been irrevocably damaged other species are also endangered as their habitat is destroyed.

Birds (Contributed by Ben Rode.)

Kenya is a paradise of birds, and campers are often in an ideal position to appreciate them. The edges of the Rift Valley lakes support a pink frosting of hundreds of thousands of flamingos, and an abundance of spoonbills, pelicans, herons, ibis, storks, waders and ducks. Meanwhile secretary birds, ostrich and bustards stride through the grasslands, as enormous eagles and vultures soar overhead. The forests hide brilliant red and green touracos and trogons, plus hornbills, owls, hoopoes and flycatchers. The coast sports a great variety of water and sea birds as well as some rare and beautiful woodland species.

A total of 1293 species of birds have been sited in Kenya, but it is not the sheer number of bird species that make Kenya so fantastic for birdwatching, rather it is the accessibility of the birds and their size, colour and variety that is unsurpassed in the world.

Many tourists who come to Kenya to see the game soon find themselves more fascinated by the birds. There are only sixty species of large mammal in Kenya and many people lose interest after seeing the big five a few times. With birds it would be more appropriate to have a big five hundred. You can always count on seeing some new birds even on the dullest of game drives.

Perhaps the uncommon saddlebilled stork typifies the magnificence of Kenya's birds. Over four feet tall with a large black, orange and yellow bill contrasting beautifully with its black and white plumage, the saddlebill never fails to send even the most dedicated big-five-game-viewing bus load of tourists scrambling for their telephotos to record its splendour. Other candidates for the magnificence award include the graceful crowned crane, the imperious martial eagle, and the stately kori bustard.

Campers who develop this interest in birds will see parts of Kenya beyond the range of most visitors, and also see the more unusual species of animal that are missed by other tourists. For example, you must walk the paths of Kakamega Forest to spot the incredible great blue touraco and a host of other central African birds in their easternmost habitat, and at the same time you will also see the blue monkey, the red-tailed monkey and perhaps a duiker. In the valleys of Kitale, while looking for spotted creeper or white-headed touraco, you might see the beautiful De Brazza monkey. Boating on Lake Baringo, to search the reed beds for goliath herons and lilly trotters, you will undoubtedly get very close to hippos and crocodiles. And only birdwatchers seeking the pygmy goose will see the uncommon view of the south face of Kilimanjaro from the shores of Lake Jipe.

Wherever you camp in Kenya, you should always take notice of the birds. They are as amazing an attraction as the mammals, and there are enough of them to keep you busy for hundreds of safaris.

For a selection of recommended field guides see the *Books* section on page 44.

BOOKS

GUIDE BOOKS

Camping Guide to Kenya fully describes all the campsites in the country, but does not even attempt to detail the many other aspects of travel in Kenya. For more information about transport, hotels, lodges, shops, restaurants, museums, places of interest, mountain climbing, backpacking, bird-watching, game-viewing, language, history, and other items not completely covered in this book, readers are advised to carry with them other more general guide books.

Nairobi, Kenya and East Africa

The Nairobi Guide   Kate Macintyre (Macmillans, Kenya)
   Complete guide to Kenya's capital city, with information on hotels, restaurants, shopping, entertainment, sport, day trips, etc.

Nairobi, Things to see and do   Alan Graham (Kenya Travel Notes)
   Slim, brief and comprehensive pamphlet providing the bare essentials required by visitors to Nairobi. Available in Nairobi.

Rough Guide to Kenya   Richard Trillo (Rough Guides, UK)
   A complete guide to Kenya covering transport, accommodation, food and places to visit. Aimed mainly at travellers with limited means, but with plenty of practical and off-beat information for visitors of all budgets. Well researched and very readable.

Insight Guide, Kenya   Mohamed Amin (Ed.) (Apa Productions, Hong Kong)
   Includes a good, if unchallenging, historical background and valuable descriptions of Kenya's numerous tribes. Lavishly illustrated with glossy photographs, but very little practical travel information. A book to read before you go.

Nation Guide to Kenya and Northern Tanzania (Marketing and Publishing Limited, Kenya)
   Includes concise information on birds and animals, and a number of suggested routes for tourists with cars. Dated now. Only available in Kenya.

East Africa, a travel survival kit   Geoff Crowther (Lonely Planet, Australia)
   Complete travel and hotel information for travellers of all but the highest budgets in Kenya, Uganda, Tanzania, Rwanda, Burundi and Eastern Zaire.

Backpacker's Africa (East and Southern)   Hilary Bradt (Bradt Publications)
   Recently updated guide to hiking and backpacking in the mountains and hills of east and southern Africa. Includes detailed chapters on the backpacking regions of Kenya, Tanzania (including Kilimanjaro), Rwanda, Burundi, Eastern Zaire, Swaziland, Lesotho, and South Africa.

Mountain Walking in Kenya   David Else (Robertson McCarta, UK)
   A selection of walking routes in the mountains and highland regions of Kenya.

Mountains of Kenya   Paul Clarke (Mountain Club of Kenya, Kenya)
   Very detailed guide to every mountain in Kenya (only brief information on Mt Kenya). Information for walkers, climbers and peak-baggers. Distributed by West Col Productions, Goring, Reading, UK.

Guide to Mount Kenya and Mount Kilimanjaro   Iain Allen (Mountain Club of Kenya, Kenya)
   Companion guide to *Mountains of Kenya*. Complete information for hikers and technical climbers on Africa's two highest peaks. Distributed by West Col Productions.

East Africa International Mountain Guide   Andrew Wielochowski (West Col Productions)
   Aimed specifically at technical climbers and mountaineers, with descriptions and grades for a selection of peaks and crags in Kenya, plus chapters on Kilimanjaro and The Ruwenzoris. Includes a brief caving section. New 1988 edition includes many hiking areas as well.

Getting there, and onward travels
Travellers and campers taking in Kenya as part of wider travels may find some of the following guides useful.

Africa on a Shoestring   Geoff Crowther (Lonely Planet, Australia)
   The near legendary 'bible' for pan-continental travellers. This book covers every country in Africa, but is so full of information that it's getting quite heavy to carry!

Sahara Handbook   Simon and Jan Glenn (Roger Lascelles, UK)
   Excellent book covering all aspects of desert driving, ideal for overlanders with vehicles heading to Kenya via the Sahara.

Backpacker's Africa (West and Central)   David Else (Bradt Publications, UK)
   Complete guide for walkers and overland travellers, covering all countries west of Zaire and south of the Sahara.

East Africa   Joe Yogerst (Roger Lascelles, UK)
Kenya and Northern Tanzania   Richard Cox (Thornton Cox, UK)
  Two useful guides for tourists visiting Tanzania after their time in Kenya.

SUGGESTED READING

A great number of books have been written about Kenya. A large library or good travel bookshop will be able to help you with titles. The list below is a selection drawn more from personal experience than from anything else.

Field Guides

Where to watch birds in Kenya   Ray Moore (Transafrica Press, Nairobi).
  A very useful guide for ornithologists, available in Nairobi bookshops.
Field Guide to the Birds of East and Central Africa   John Williams (Collins, UK)
  Makes birding in Kenya even more of a pleasure. Invaluable, although the colours are sometimes misleadingly dull!

A Field Guide to the Mammals of Africa   T. Haltenorth and H. Diller (Collins, UK)
  Another useful guide for campers on safari, whose interest in Kenya's animals stretches beyond the Big Five.

East African Birds   Sapra Safari Guides No.6, C.A.W. Guggisberg (Mount Kenya Sundries, Kenya)
  A more portable bird guide than Collins', but sometimes difficult to find. Only available in Kenya.

A Field Guide to the National Parks of East Africa   J.G. Williams (Collins, UK)
  Good information on all the national parks, although dated in places, with maps, and animal and bird checklists.

Health

Travellers' Health   Dr Richard Dawood (O.U.P., UK)
  Detailed.

Practical Guides

The Traveller's Handbook   Melissa Shales (Ed) (Trade and Travel Publications, UK)
  An encyclopaedic guide to all aspects of travel for anyone on the move around the world.

The Backpacker's Manual Cameron McNeish (Oxford Illustrated Press, UK)

A complete guide to walking, backpacking and camping techniques. Not aimed at African travellers, but most of the information it contains applies to hills and mountains in all parts of the world. Invaluable preparation reading for first-time campers and backpackers, with plenty of useful tips for the old hands too.

Stay Alive in the Desert K.E.M. Melville (Roger Lascelles, UK)
Explorer's Handbook Christina Dodwell (Hodder and Stoughton, UK)

Desert and jungle survival for intrepid travellers.

Swahili Dictionary Teach Yourself Books

General Reading

Out of Africa Karen Blixen (Penguin, UK)
White Mischief James Fox (Penguin, UK)
The Flame Trees of Thika Elspeth Huxley (Penguin, UK)

Classic colonial stuff to get you in a romantic, sentimental mood.

Kenya Diary (1902–1906) Richard Meinertzhagen (Eland, UK)

More classic stuff, but in no way sentimental. The real, and very dark, side of colonialism.

Petals of Blood Ngugi wa Thiog'o, African Writers Series
Going Down the River Road Meja Mwangi, African Writers Series (Heinemann, UK)

Not romantic, but impressively evocative, modern Kenyan masterpieces. Try any of the works in this series.

Memories of Kenya Arnold Curtis (Evans, UK)
The Kenya Pioneers E. Trzebinski (Heinemann, UK)

Readable accounts of Kenya's early years.

Turn Left, the Rifts have Risen A. Cameron Gilg (RAC, UK)
Journey to the Jade Sea John Hillaby (Paladin, UK)
Jupiter's Travels Ted Simon (Penguin,UK)
A Hitchhiker's Guide to Africa and Arabia David Hatcher Childress (The Chicago Review Press, USA)

A selection of travellers passing through Kenya; journeys by Morris 8 in 1933, by camel in 1962, and by motorbike and thumb in the seventies. More good reading to get you in the mood.

Different Drums   Michael Wood (Century Hutchinson Ltd, UK)
The Tree Where Man Was Born   Peter Matthiessen (Picador, UK)

Fine descriptions and thoughts on a changing continent. Without being sentimental both books discuss the effect of colonialism and post-colonialism on isolated African peoples. *Different Drums* is written with knowledge and insight by one of Kenya's leading medical figures, and is beautifully illustrated throughout with photos by David Coulson. *The Tree Where Man Was Born* is an account of the author's journeys through Kenya and Northern Tanzania and his intimate encounters with little known groups of people.

The Marsh Lions   Brian Jackman and Jonathon Scott (Elm Tree Books, UK)

Story of a many years' worth of research compacted into 12 months in the Masai Mara studying a group of lions. An opportunity to learn something of the interaction between animals and their environment. Illustrated throughout with drawings and colour photographs.

If you have trouble tracing any of the guide-books described above contact:
Edward Stanford Ltd, 12–14 Long Acre, Covent Garden, London WC2E 9LP;
The Travel Bookshop, 13 Blenheim Crescent, London W11 2EE.

For a very comprehensive range of Natural History books by mail order contact the Natural History Book Service, 2 Wills Rd, Totnes, Devon TQ9 9XN, UK, Tel: (0803) 865913.

Trailfinders (see address in *Getting There*), has a well stocked Information Centre with a library of travel books and guides that customers with reservations are free to use.

MAPS

Maps of Kenya

Until about ten years ago the Survey of Kenya produced a very complete range of maps covering the whole country, including mountain regions and national parks, which was freely available. Many maps are now out of print or no longer available to the general public.

Kenya and Northern Tanzania, Route Map   Scale 1:1,000,000, Sheet No. SK 81 (Survey of Kenya, Kenya)

This map has been officially withdrawn, and can now only be found in shops with stocks remaining. Most recently re-printed in 1972, some of the roads shown on this map have been newly surfaced or fallen into dis-use. Various road classification numbers have also been changed. But for locating smaller *centres* and villages, and for topographical detail, this map is excellent.

Because the Survey of Kenya *Route Map* has become harder to find, various other companies have produced maps, aiming to fill the gap. These include:

Kenya   Scale 1:1,100,000, Nelles Maps (Nelles Verlag, Germany).

Very clear to read, but the road network has been copied from the *Route Map* resulting in inevitable errors. The map is over-printed with useful tourist information.

Kenya Tourist Map   Scale 1:1,750,000 (Macmillans, Kenya)

Limited detail and altitude shading makes this map clear to read and useful for route planning. On reverse is printed maps of Central Nairobi, Mombasa and Nairobi National Park, and a list of places of interest.

Kenya Road Map   Scale 1:1,500,000 (Freytag and Berndt, Austria)

Cluttered and difficult to read. Limited topographical detail.

Also available:

Shell Map of Kenya   (Shell Kenya Limited, Kenya)

Produced in Kenya. Difficult to obtain.

Kenya   Scale 1:1,250,000, Bartholomews World Travel Map (John Bartholomew & Son Ltd, UK)

Insufficient topographical information. Lack of distinction between roads of varying surfaces.

We have found that no single map of Kenya is completely correct, or ideal for all uses. It is advisable to use two or three maps together.

Note when map reading, that often railway stations are marked on the map which may be some kilometres away from the village, or *centre*, of the same name.

Parks and Reserves

Survey of Kenya also produce a series of maps covering most of the frequently visited national parks and reserves. These are infrequently updated and reprinted, so can sometimes be difficult to find.

Maps include: *Amboseli*, *Tsavo West*, *Tsavo East*, *Meru*, *Samburu and Buffalo Springs*, *Marsabit* and *Shimba Hills*.

Other maps of parks and reserves include:

Amboseli National Park Map and *Masai Mara National Reserve Map*   (Macmillans, Kenya)
Very recently produced, clear to read, and as detailed as any game park map can be.

Masai Mara   (Rowyena Enterprises, Kenya)

Mountains

Survey of Kenya maps of the Mount Kenya peak area and the Mount Kenya National Park (reprinted in 1979) are unavailable in Kenya. The only map available is:

Mount Kenya, Map and Guide   Scale 1:50,000, Andrew Wielochowski and Mark Savage (East Africa Mountain Guides), Distributed by West Col Productions (address below).

A clear four-colour map of Mount Kenya showing all main routes on the mountain, with insets showing the wider national park area and the central peaks. The reverse contains detailed information about routes, huts, porters, flora and fauna, etc.

For wider travels

Africa, Central and South   Scale 1:4,000,000, Sheet No.955 (Michelin, France)

The Michelin Maps are still, without doubt, the best large scale maps of Africa. Highly recommended for long distance travelling. Also in the same scale: *Africa, North and West* and *Africa, North-East*.

Africa, East   Scale 1:2,500,000, Bartholomew World Travel Map (John Bartholomew & Son Ltd, UK)

Lacking sufficient detail for anything more than main road travelling. And even then, many of the main roads, as denoted by the red lines on the map, are no more than mud tracks, or completely non-existent.

Survey of Kenya maps may be available in the public Map Office (next to the Conference Centre) on Harambee Avenue in Nairobi, but an official letter stating your reasons for wanting to buy a map may be required. A letter saying you are a tourist should be enough, but the situation may change at any time. Even if you do get a letter it's quite likely that the Map Office will not be able to provide the map you require as stocks are often low.

In recent years it has become increasingly difficult to buy maps in Kenya, especially more detailed maps of the mountain areas described in this book. Driving maps of the whole country, or of specific national parks and reserves can still be found in various bookshops. Try the Nation Bookshop next to the New Stanley Hotel, or any of the map and stationery shops along Standard Street. The shop at the National Museum also has a good selection.

McCarta Ltd, 122 Kings Cross Road, London WC1X 9DS, Tel: 01 278 8276, stocks maps to all parts of the world and has a wide selection of maps of Kenya and Africa. For more specialised maps and mountain guides of Kenya contact West Col Productions, Goring, Reading, UK.

GLOSSARY

An explanation of some Swahili words and other terms used in Kenya that appear in this book.

Matatu   Public minibus
Hoteli   Basic restaurant
Boarding and Lodging   Basic hotel (Often shortened to *Lodging* or *B&L*)
Duka   Small shop
Askari   Guard, watchman
Mzungu   White person
Chai   Tea
Soda   Any fizzy drink
Pombe   Home made beer
Shamba   Plot of ground, smallholding
Panga   Large cutting knife, machete
Centre   Collection of huts and dukas, village
Murram road   Graded dirt road
Drift   Ford
Bluff   Cliff, outcrop
Tarn   Mountain lake
Dam   Artificial lake
Col   Low point between hills
Cairn   Pile of stones used for way-marking
Gof   Crater (used in the north)

Other useful words
Jambo   Hello
Habari?   How are you?
Mzuri   Fine
Karibu   Welcome
Asanti   Thankyou
Sana   Very much
Ngapi?   How much?
Wapi?   Where?
Choo   Toilet

For more Kiswahili words read *The Swahili Dictionary* Teach Yourself Books. *The Rough Guide to Kenya* has a good glossary and introduction to basic Kiswahili.

Abbreviations used in this book
ppn   per person per night
psw   per site per week
4WD   four wheel drive
2WD   Two wheel drive

MAPS IN THIS BOOK

The maps in this book are as accurate as sketch maps can be. They are intended for guidance only and you are advised to use published maps as well. Note, however, that some published maps are also incorrect in certain respects. For more details see the *Maps* section.

In some areas, too many minor tracks exist to show with accuracy on the maps, so only the main tracks are drawn. Similarly, on town maps only main streets are shown, and on some maps of parks and reserves only the developed areas (which usually include the campsites) are drawn.

When map reading, especially in remote areas and national parks, remember that the pattern of roads can change; routes can be affected by seasonal factors as surfaces are damaged and bridges washed away, roads can be regraded or tarred, or tracks become disused and overgrown. So try to orientate using prominent features such as hills, rivers and lodges.

Note that some names have variable spellings and are not consistent between maps. For example, *L* and *R* are often interchanged, and the prefix *Ol* may or may not be included.

It is suggested that readers use a coloured pen to mark on the maps distances and times described in the text. For clarity these have not been shown. This would be particularly useful on maps on Mount Elgon and Mount Kenya.

KEY

For all maps in this book.

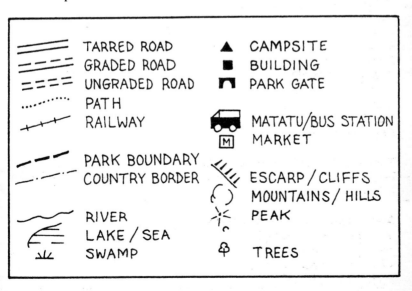

NAIROBI

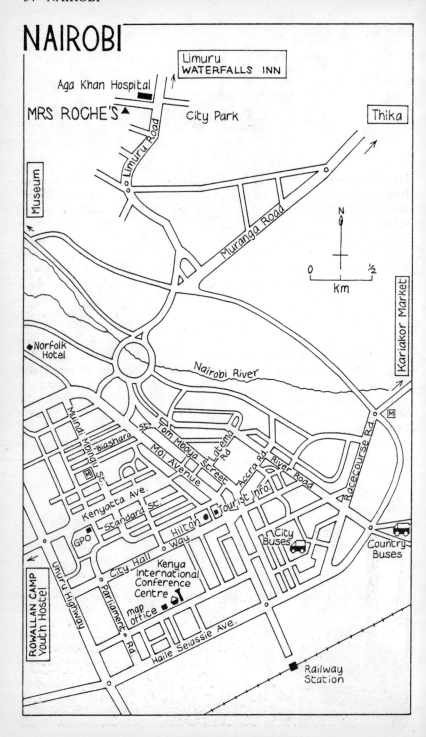

Chapter 7

Nairobi

Nairobi, the capital city of Kenya, is where most visitors first arrive and from where they begin to organise their journeys and expeditions around the country. Other visitors may have already arranged camping safaris from their home country, but will still be staying in Nairobi before or after their trip.

Nairobi has a limited selection of campsites, which are fully described below, but for the first night or two newcomers may prefer to stay in a hotel. Nairobi has a wide range of hotels catering for all budgets. Most general guide books contain detailed hotel information (see the *Books* section), or ask for details at the Tourist Information Office outside the Hilton Hotel in central Nairobi. There are a number of mid-range hotels around the city centre, while the budget hotels tend to be located in the Latema Road/River Road area to the north of Tom Mboya Street. The Iqbal Hotel on Latema Road is the best value for money but is often full. Alternatives include the nearby New Kenya Lodge or Sunrise Lodge.

Most visitors arriving in Kenya will find the following information useful. For more comprehensive details ask at the central Tourist Information Office. Generally of more use is one of the free magazines *What's On* and *Tourist's Kenya*, or the small booklet *Nairobi, Things to See and Do* available for 5/− at most hotels and book shops.

Shops Most shops in Nairobi are open 0800 – 1730 Monday – Saturday. A limited number of shops are open on Sunday.

Banks A wide selection of banks change travellers cheques and foreign currency. Exchange rates and commission costs vary. Opening hours also vary but most banks are open 0900–1300 h. Some open earlier, others later. If the banks are closed, it is usually possible to change money at large hotels.

Post Post Offices keep similar hours to shops. The *poste restante* service is based at Nairobi's main post office (the GPO) on Kenyatta Avenue. Letters cost 1/– inside Kenya, 5/– to the UK, 7/– to the USA. Aerogrammes cost 3/– worldwide.

Telephones Public booths can be found at many points in Nairobi. International calls can be made from the GPO or large hotels.

Chemists/Pharmacies Most medicinal items are available from Nairobi's chemists, although prices for imported items are higher than in Europe or America.

Doctors Embassies provide visitors with a list of recommended doctors and hospitals.

Photographics Film supplies are easy to find in a number of good photography shops, and only slightly more expensive than in Europe or America. Printing quality is variable. The following shop can be recommended: Camera Experts, Mama Ngina St, near the Hilton; Tel: 337750, for Kodak developing, spares and repairs.

and white developing and printing; Camera Experts, on Mama Ngina Street, near the Hilton Hotel, Tel: 337750, for Kodak developing, spares and repairs.

Market Nairobi's central City Market, between Muindi Mbingu and Koinange Streets, has fruit, vegetables, meat and fish, and a collection of stalls selling baskets, carvings and other tourist artifacts.

Launderette If your hotel does not have a laundry service, the launderette at Westlands Shopping Centre is reasonable.

Newspapers Kenya has three daily papers in English: *The Nation*, *The Standard* and *The Kenya Times*. Most foreign newspapers are available at main news-stands in the city centre.

Youth Hostel The Nairobi hostel, on Ralph Bunche Rd between the Kenyatta Ave extension and Valley Rd, is very popular with travellers. Facilities include a kitchen, common room/library, hot showers, shop and gear storage. A bed costs 60ppn for IYFH members.

Camping is not permitted at the youth hostel, and unofficial camping of any sort in Nairobi cannot be recommended. Although Uhuru Park and the other green spaces in the city may seem pleasant enough, robberies and muggings are not unknown even during the day and should be especially avoided at night.

MRS ROCHE'S

Mrs Roche's house, in the suburb of Parklands, has been a travellers' haven for many years, a pleasant retreat from the noise and fumes of Nairobi while still only a short matatu ride away from the city centre. You have a choice of rooms in the house or beds in the dormitory, or tents can be pitched on the lawn.

Mrs Roche's has always been used by travellers with vehicles but in more recent years trans-African overland trucks with up to twenty passengers have used the garden and drive during their stop in Nairobi. Large groups of people can disturb the laid back atmosphere of Mrs Roche's, and the increasing number of vehicles (often undergoing repair or even major rebuilds) turns the lawn into something like a used car lot.

For all this, Mrs Roche's is still very popular and the only place in Nairobi for travellers without vehicles to pitch a tent in relative safety.

Position   Mrs Roche's is opposite the Aga Khan Hospital on Third Parklands Avenue, off the Limuru Road. Car drivers coming from the city centre should follow the Muranga Road out of town over the Nairobi River. After 1.5 km the Limuru Road branches left from the Muranga Road, then after a further 2 km City Park is on the right. Third Parklands Avenue is on the left.

Buses run from the city centre along the Limuru Road, but matatus are quicker, more frequent, and easier to find, although often of dubious safety. The best place to find matatus going to Third Parklands Avenue is outside Nation House at the end of Tom Mboya Street. Ask for the Aga Khan Hospital, although most of the matatu drivers know Mrs Roche's.

Cost   40/– ppn for camping. Parking: 10/– per car.
Facilities   Water, toilets, hot showers (sometimes), clothes washing platform. No open fires allowed. No kitchen, but plenty of shops, dukas and hotelis nearby. Gear storage: 20/– per bag per week.
Security   Fence and askari. No reports of large scale robberies, but don't leave cameras and other valuables lying around.
Dormitory   50/– ppn.

A campsite is signposted at the entrance to the City Park on Limuru Road near Mrs Roche's. This sign has been here for many years, but as yet no campsite has been built.

ROWALLAN CAMP

Rowallan Camp is the national centre for Kenya's scout movement, but the campsite can also be used by tourists. The camp is in an area of forest outside the city centre and, although it can be reached by public transport and walking, it's more suitable for campers with their own vehicles. Many long distance travellers prefer to park here when Mrs Roche's becomes too crowded.

Scouts from all over Kenya come to camp here and the site can get busy in the school holidays. You can escape the crowds by heading deeper into the surrounding forest, but leaving your tent and vehicle unattended would not be safe.

Position   Rowallan Camp is about 7 km from Nairobi city centre, between the shanty town of Kibera and Jamhuri Park, Nairobi's international showground. From the city centre take Kenyatta Avenue up the hill, then Ngong Road towards the residential suburb of Karen. Turn left towards Kibera and pass to the north of the shanty town, keeping on the tar road. After Kibera the road drops, crosses a stream, then climbs towards the forest. At the signs 'World Scout Bureau' and 'Rowallan Camp' turn left on to a dirt track to reach the camp buildings after 0.5 km.

Cost   20/− ppn.

Facilities   Water, toilets and showers (not in good condition). Small shop, swimming pool. The wardens office is usually open during the day (Tel: 568111).

Security   It's safer to pitch your tent within sight of the warden's office and other camp buildings.

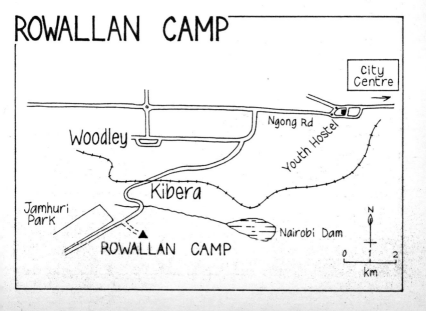

WATERFALLS INN

Waterfalls Inn is a picnic site and riding centre, with a restaurant and bar, some cottages and a campsite, situated in the farming area of Kamonde to the north-west of Nairobi. The site is built on a hill-top overlooking the farmland and surrounding tea-plantations, with views of the city, the Ngong Hills, and (on a very clear day) Kilimanjaro. The picturesque waterfalls are a short walk away.

The site is particularly popular at weekends and during the school holidays when families from Nairobi come out for the day, but at other times it is usually quiet and peaceful. Once again, access is the main problem for travellers without vehicles, but for motorised campers the site is safer, better equipped, and in more pleasant surroundings than either Mrs Roche's or Rowallan Camp.

Position   The Waterfalls Inn is about 30 km north-west from Nairobi city-centre near the town of Limuru. Car drivers coming from the city centre should follow the directions for Mrs Roche's to reach the Limuru Road, then continuing to Muthaiga Roundabout. Continue on the Limuru Road for 7 km to Ruaka then fork right, still following the 'old' Limuru Road (also called Banana Road, officially numbered D407/D105). Follow this tarred road for 14.5 km and turn right by the Kenchic factory, also on to a tarred road. After 1 km turn right on to a dirt track, which winds up the hill for a further 1 km to the Waterfalls Inn.

Drivers coming from the direction of Naivasha and Nakuru can turn off the main A104 at the junction with the C62. Follow the C62 for about 7 km then turn left towards Tigoni, pass the small lake and the entrance to Limuru Country Club, then at Tigoni Police Station, turn right onto the D105. Follow this road for 5 km until the Kenchic factory, turn left here and follow the directions above.

Bus 116 runs directly but infrequently from the central bus station to Kamonde. Alternatively take bus or matutu 106 to Banana, then another from there to Kimonde. Ask to be dropped at the Kenchic factory. Limuru Girls School is another well known landmark.

Cost   30/− ppn (Picnic Campsite), 40/− ppn (Cottage Campsite).
Facilities   Picnic Campsite: Water, toilets, cold showers.
Cottage Campsite: More secluded. Water, toilets and hot showers in the cottages. Lights. Fire place, firewood. Benches and tables.
Meals available at the restaurant. Small shop on site, and the nearest duka 5 minutes walk away at the school.
Security   Fence, askaris, lights.
Cottage   350/− double.
Entry to picnic site for non-campers: 100/− per car.
Bookings/Enquiries   Mr Khalid Butt, Tel: (0154) 40672

WATERFALLS INN

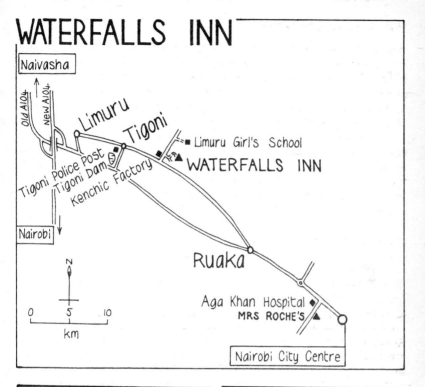

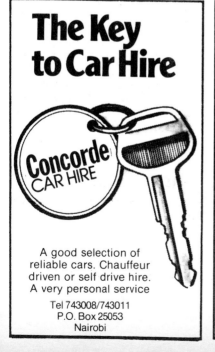

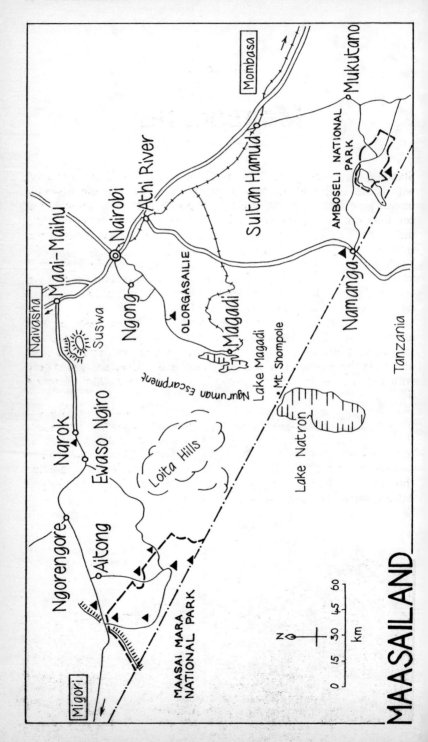

Chapter 8

Maasailand

Standing tall, proudly dressed in red robes, and elaborately decorated with beads and paint the Maasai people make popular picture-book images. For visitors the Maasai tribe is probably the best known, and certainly the most photographed, of all the tribes in Africa. Unlike many other groups in Kenya the Maasai have largely rejected the trappings of modern civilisation and kept to their traditional way of life. Their society is based around their cattle; cows are a highly prized symbol of wealth and status. Consequently the Maasai homelands are the wide grassy plains of northern Tanzania and southern Kenya, that have always provided unlimited grazing for the herds.

These grasslands are also the natural home for millions of wild animals − gazelle, wildebeest, zebra, giraffe, elephant, buffalo, chee-tah, leopard and lion − and historically the Maasai and their herds lived alongside these animals in peaceful co-existence. Even so, armed only with a spear, a warrior would protect his family's cows from a hunting lion.

During colonial times the unlimited game in Maasailand attracted hunters anxious for trophies, and the wildlife in this region became in danger of being completely destroyed. This led to the creation of national parks and reserves, established to protect the wildlife and to preserve their habitats. Today, armed with cameras rather than guns, thousands of tourists every year visit the two main parks of Kenyan Maasailand at Amboseli and Maasai Mara.

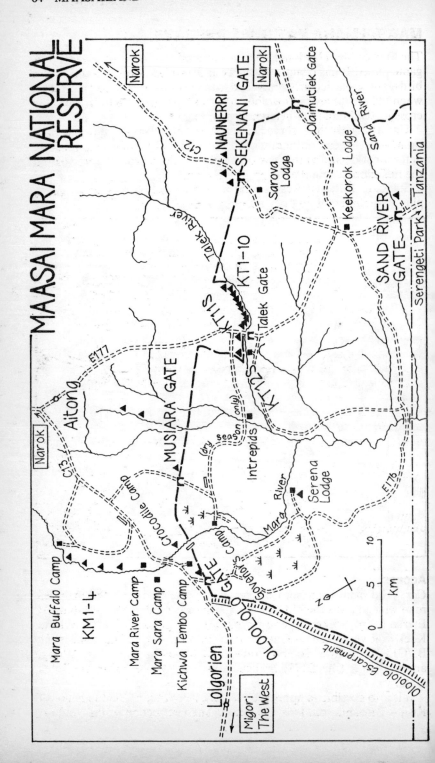

MAASAI MARA NATIONAL RESERVE.

The Maasai Mara National Reserve is one of East Africa's most famous game parks. It has beautiful scenery and a wide variety of animals and birds, and is particularly renowned for the annual wildebeest migration when the great herds follow the rains and fresh grass up from Tanzania crossing the Mara river in a spectacular manner.

Unfortunately the reserve has become so popular in recent years that safari vehicles can outnumber the lions, but with good map-reading, determination and a little time, it is still possible to avoid the crowds and the ridiculous 'cat in the car-park' situation.

Standard National Reserve entrance fees are payable at all gates, plus a surcharge of 50/- per person per day.

Access

Car The main route into the reserve is via Narok, on the main B3 road which leaves the old Nairobi – Naivasha road at Maai-Mahiu. At Ewaso Ngiro, 15 km beyond Narok, are crossroads: left is the C12 to Keekorok via Sekenani Gate, tarred for a further 40 km; right is the B3/C13 to Kichwa Tembo Lodge and Oloololo Gate. At Aitong, another track (the E177) branches off towards Keekorok via Talek Gate.

It is also possible to approach the park from Migori (on the main A1 Kisii – Tanzania road) via Lolgorien. The last section of this route is very steep (4WD is needed even in the dry season) and the road is seldom used.

Other gates into the reserve are: Musiara Gate, near Oloololo Gate on the east side of the Mara River; Olaimutiek Gate, near Sekenani Gate, at the eastern edge of the reserve; Sand River Gate, on the southern boundary of the reserve which is also the border between Kenya and Tanzania. Only vehicles coming in from the Serengeti National Park in Tanzania can enter at this last gate.

All these roads into the park are very rough and frequently impassable after the rains.

When driving in the park, remember that only two bridges cross the Mara River which effectively divides the park in two: the northern Mara River Bridge is near Kichwa Tembo Lodge; the southern Mara New Bridge is on the E176 main park track between Oloololo Gate and Keekorok.

Bus/Hitch   Buses and matatus go as far as Narok, and you will have to hitch from there. Hundreds of safari minibuses will pass you by, and tourists in their own cars with seats to spare are very rare. It is possible to hitch a ride with a supply lorry to one of the lodges, but after that you may get stuck again.

Coming in from the west there are occasional matatus to Lolgorien from Migori, or from Kisii, but after that the chance of a lift is even less than if you are coming in from Narok.

The Maasai are very hospitable. When we were hitching down to Narok we got invited by some young men we met to come and sleep the night in their manyatta. This would be an unusual experience and it was already getting dark so we agreed. We couldn't make out much, but the manyatta was a collection of small mud huts, square with flat roofs, surrounded by a strong fence made of branches and thorn bush. After eating (I'm not sure exactly what we ate) it was time to sleep. The cattle had already been brought inside the fence and the smell was overpowering. It was surprisingly warm inside the hut we were given, the thick mud walls must act as insulation. The herd surrounding the huts kept them warm too. But the biggest problem was the flies. Attracted by the cows and kept active by the warmth there were millions of them buzzing around our faces, getting in our ears and noses. For a while I tried to get away from them inside my sleeping bag, but that was too hot, and when I came up again it was even worse. An interesting experience but not really enjoyable. The next night we camped! (Arik Orbach and Limoh Rozen, Israel)

CAMPING

Officially, twenty-five campsites are located in the Maasai Mara Reserve area, but no single map marks them all. Some sites are very difficult to find, especially those north of the reserve in the area between C13 and the E177 roads in from Aitong.

A government plan allows the Maasai to earn money from campers. For sites inside the park you pay at the gate for the number of nights you intend staying. Then at the site you pay for a Maasai askari, and a supply of water and firewood, if required. At sites outside the park boundary Maasai will arrive to collect the camp fee directly.

Officially, all campsite reservations have to be made at the National Parks Headquaters at the Main (Langata Road) Gate of Nairobi National Park, but in practice you can arrive at any public campsite without pre-booking. It may be necessary to reserve special sites, but the requirements are unclear. If you require a special campsite in Maasai Mara check the situation at the Nairobi Headquarters first or contact the warden at the park directly.

Cost 50/- ppn. Special campsites 300/- ppn.

The regulations concerning camping in the reserve are currently undergoing review, so be prepared for price and site changes in 1989/90.

Booking The Warden, Maasai Mara National Reserve, PO Box 60, Narok.

Some of the campsites in the Maasai Mara are organised by the Maasai tribesmen themselves. The idea is they can earn money from their land. This would be fine, but some of them seem to get a little anxious about bringing in the money. At our site on the Talek River we were constantly pestered by Maasai demanding extra money for firewood and water we didn't want, or for their services as guards. But we met the cheekiest of them all on the way back to Nairobi when we stopped to give a young Maasai boy a lift in the car. After carrying him for only a few kilometres he told us to stop the car, and then as he got out he said we'd have to pay him some money because we'd given him a ride! (Ady and Dudy, Israel)

Oloololo Gate Public Campsite

Camping is allowed on a patch of grass behind the workers' houses just outside the gate.

Facilities Pit toilet, water and a small duka nearby.

Musiara Gate Public Campsite

For overnight stops camping is near the workers' houses. For longer stays ask to camp under nearby trees, which are blissfully free of baboons and tourists, although the occasional group of elephants may wander through.

Facilities Pit toilet, no water.

Crocodile Camp

This is a private campsite for the American NOLS organisation. It is outside the reserve on the opposite bank of the river to the Kichwa Tembo sites.

Mara Serena Lodge Public Campsite

Position This campsite is to the west of the Mara River near the lodge and the park sub-HQ.

Facilities Pit toilets, water.

Mara River Special Campsites

These four campsites (numbered KM1 to KM4) are outside the reserve in a Maasai concession area. They are sited along a stretch of river bank under shady trees. Hippos wander at will in the night. These sites are popular with middle range safari companies so may be booked up in the tourist seasons.

Position   The KM campsites are on the east bank of the Mara River, north of the Mara Bridge.
Facilities   None.
Security   Maasai askari, if required. Fee negotiable.

There is another area which has been used by campers south of these campsites, near Mara River Camp, and conveniently near the road. Drive down the track nearly to the entrance of the camp and then turn sharp left up a faint track.

Talek River Public Campsites

These ten public sites (numbered KT1 to KT10) line the picturesque north bank of the Talek River outside the park boundary in the Maasai concession area. There is a Maasai manyatta nearby. Lions, elephants and buffalo frequent the area along with other, less worrying, species.

Position   The KT campsites are to the east of Talek Gate, just north of the park boundary.
Facilities   Each site has a pit toilet, none has water. Water from the river is alright for washing, but take your own drinking water.
Security   Maasai askari, if required. Fee negotiable.

Talek Gate Campsite

Formally designated a 'special' campsite (number KT11S), this site is now open to the public.

Position   To the west of the main track, on the north bank of the river.
Facilities   Pit toilet, cooking shelter, water from the gate or KT12S.
Security   Maasai askari, if required. Fee negotiable.

Fig Tree Special Campsite

This special site, numbered KT12S, is situated in a pleasant spot on the north bank of the river to the west of the gate and Telek Gate Campsite (KT11S). There are numerous tracks in this area; if in doubt keep near the river.

Facilities   Pit toilet, rain water tank, showers (30/- extra).
Security   Baboons can be a problem. Maasai askari, if required.

Sekenani Gate Public Campsites

These campsites, numbered 1 – 4, are on the right (west) side of the track, about 0.5 km before the gate.

Facilities   None, water from stream.
Security   Maasai askaris, if required. Fee negotiable.

Sand River Gate Public Campsite
The site is popular with budget safari companies from Nairobi and with overland tours coming up from Tanzania. The grass can be high after the rains, but spaces for tents are cut.
Position   The campsite is outside the park on the south side of the river.
Facilities   Pit toilets, no water.

Naunerri Special Campsite
A very pleasant site, in a clump of trees, on a hillside about 0.5 km to the left (east) of the main track, about 3 km before the gate.
Facilities   Pit toilet, no water.

Note   The once popular Keekorok Lodge Public Campsite has been closed due to erosion caused by overuse.

NAROK

Narok is a small town roughly halfway between Nairobi and the Maasai Mara National Reserve. There is a market, a petrol station, several shops, and a campsite which makes a convenient stopping-off place for campers heading to or from the reserve.

MEMBER'S CLUB
The Narok Member's Club is a small bar set in a garden amongst trees. Banda accommodation is available. Tents can be pitched on the clean grassy site which is near the bar, and can be noisy at night.
Position   Aiming towards Maasai Mara, 0.5 km outside Narok, the club is signposted on the right (north) side of the road.
Cost   100/- per tent per night.
Facilities   Water, cold showers, toilets.
Security   Fence and askari.
Bandas   100/- ppn.

The baboons in Maasai Mara are getting really clever. They are totally unafraid of humans and will come right up to your tent if you're not keeping a constant look out. A group of us from Nairobi spent Christmas camping at Keekorok, and had taken all the luxurious items we could fit in; tables, chairs, cool box, beer...

We thought everything was safe, but two particularly cheeky baboons came close and stole some bottles of whisky and gin! It could have been a real tragedy! We chased after the pesky beasts and fortunately they dropped the bottles. This was lucky, as it would've been a long way back to Nairobi to stock up the drinks cabinet again! (Elizabeth Slinn, Nairobi)

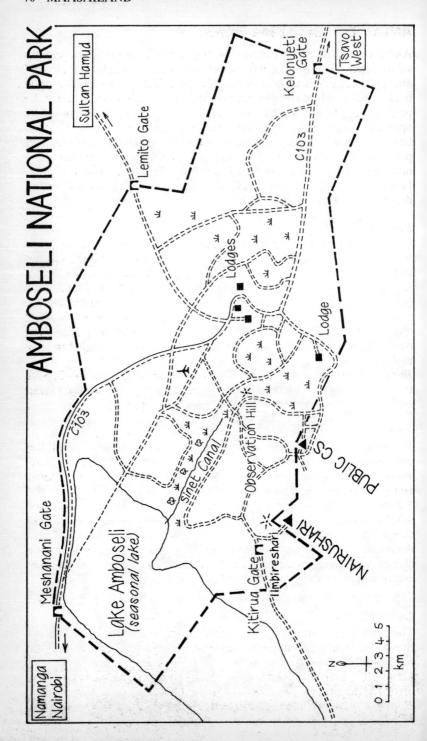

AMBOSELI NATIONAL PARK

Amboseli is particularly famous for its elephants, and is a very popular safari destination especially for short term visitors as it is near Nairobi and the visibility is usually good. The backdrop of the snow-capped peak of Kilimanjaro compensates for the rather sparse landscape in the park itself. During the dry season the park takes on a semi-desert appearance. Scientists suggest that rising salt levels leads to the death of trees and bushes while foraging by the park's large herds of elephant prevents regrowth. Serious erosion is also caused by the ever-increasing numbers of cars and minibuses carrying visitors around the park. However tempting it is to stalk that rhino just a little bit further, all drivers should stay on the official tracks.

Access

Car   The main route into the park is along the C103 from Namanga, on the Nairobi – Arusha (Tanzania) road, via Meshanani Gate. This road is badly corrugated and potholed in places. It is also possible to enter via Kelonyeti Gate on the C103 from the Chyulu Gate in Tsavo West National Park. Lemito Gate is closed at present because the road is impassably potholed. When it's open this road joins with the C102 'pipeline road' from Sultan Hamud on the main Nairobi – Mombasa road. The track from Namanga to Kitirua Gate goes through Tanzania and is not used.

Bus/Hitch   Buses from Nairobi go as far as Namanga, but you will have to hitch from here. This will be difficult as most of the vehicles are safari company minibuses, and you cannot walk in the park.

At dusk Amboseli's scenery is quintessentially African. Silhouettes of acacias and thorn trees stand before a technicolour sunset. In the last moments of light the snows on Kili turn deep pink. From the bush come the night noises of animals on the move; hyenas laugh, baboons chatter and if you're lucky you may get to hear the roar of a lion...

Nice park, shame about the erosion. There are so many cars and minibuses chasing the animals that grass in Amboseli is becoming a rare commodity. I think in a few years time it will not be possible to visit Amboseli. Either the park will be completely closed to tourists, giving it a chance to recover, or else there'll be nothing left to see except a huge empty dust bowl. (Sharon Newcombe, Canada)

CAMPING

The campsites in Amboseli are run by Maasai communities. Although these are technically outside the park boundary, they can only be reached via the park.

Cost   30/– ppn. Special campsites 1000/– psw. Pay Maasai direct on arrival at the sites.

Booking   The Warden, Amboseli National Park, PO Box 18, Namanga.

Public Campsite

This is Amboseli's only public campsite, also called the Group Ranch. It is large, but popular with low-budget camping safari companies and so can get crowded and noisy at times.

Position   The public campsite is outside the park boundary to the south-west of Observation Hill.

Facilities   Two pit toilets, some shade, firewood. The water tank is filled from a borehole and said to be drinkable. The water supply is not always reliable in which case water has to be collected from one of the lodges. The campsite office sells beers and sodas if they have been brought from the lodge.

Security   For independent campers a personal Maasai askari can be arranged.

Nairushari Special Campsite

This site is used mostly by the high-budget safari companies, but if it is booked the local Maasai can arrange another equally secluded site, provided you pay the usual reservation fee.

Position   To reach this site pass through the south-west corner of the park near Ilmbireshari Hill.

Facilities   Shade, firewood. Collect water from the public site or take your own.

When we camped at Amboseli we had the campsite almost to ourselves. It had been a long day's game viewing so we all bedded down early. We were woken suddenly by a loud clattering coming from the pile of saucepans our cook had left to drain. I stuck my head out to have a look. There in the moonlight only a few yards from the tent was a huge hyena. It heard me undoing the zip of the tent and instead of running off it turned to look at me. After what seemed an age it turned round and slunk slowly off into the dark.

After that we lay awake for some time, starting at every noise, but must have drifted off to sleep eventually.

The next noise to wake us was the sound of wood snapping and bushes being shaken. This time it took me longer to summon up the courage, but I steeled myself to undo the zip again. At first I couldn't see anything then realised I was looking straight at the dark side of an elephant! It was so close that even in the dark I could see the wrinkles in its skin and hear the gurgling of its stomach. I could only watch quietly and hope that the driver's assurances about the dexterity of elephants was true.

The driver and cook sat over their early morning coffee and cigarettes, unruffled by the animals' night visits. It's quite a common occurrence apparently. Just another Amboseli night...(Joseph Flaherty, USA)

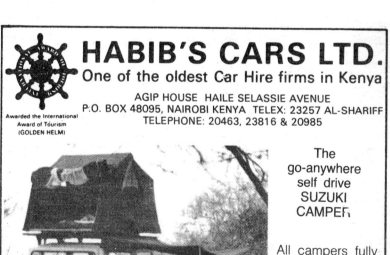

NAMANGA

Namanga is the border town on the road between Nairobi and Arusha in Tanzania, and also the last town on the main route into Amboseli National Park. There is a petrol station, a hotel, a bar, some dukas and a great number of souvenir stalls selling the usual Maasai bric-a-brac. Tourists waiting to cross the border or filling with petrol are besieged by Maasai people selling their wares. Photos are not allowed.

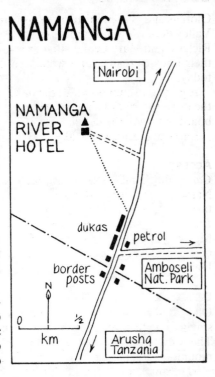

Access

Car Namanga is about 120 km south of Nairobi on the main road to Tanzania. This road is tarred all the way.

Bus/Hitch Buses run from Nairobi to the border, or direct to Arusha. There's plenty of traffic on this road, and hitching to Namanga or on to Tanzania is no problem.

NAMANGA RIVER HOTEL

This is an old colonial-style hotel with a vaguely Bavarian character just a few hundred metres away from the border. Camping is at the side of the hotel buildings in amongst chalet-style bandas on a shady lawn.

Position The Namanga River Hotel is 200 m west of the main Nairobi – Namanga road 500 m before the border. Follow the rusty signs.

Cost 30/– ppn.

Facilities Water, toilets, showers, bar. Dukas in Namanga.

Security Fence and askaris.

Bandas Around 300/– single.

We were camping at Amboseli. It was a clear day and I was trying to take a picture of the tents with Kilimanjaro as a background. I saw an elephant some way off and presumed it would keep its distance. I wanted to include it in the photo though, so I waited with my zoom lens ready. As I watched, the elephant walked slowly and deliberately towards the campsite. As it began to completely fill the zoom all thoughts of a photo were forgotten and we ran to the car. The elephant just strolled through the middle of the site and didn't stop. This made us a lot happier. Shame about the photo though! (Elizabeth Slinn)

OLORGASAILIE

Olorgasailie is a prehistoric site on the hot, sparsely populated, Rift Valley floor a few hours drive out of Nairobi. The famous archaeologists Richard and Mary Leakey first excavated here in the 1940s but many of their finds, spread over a wide area, have been left for visitors to see today.

A good museum provides the background to the site before you go to the digs. Informative guides will show you around and well positioned boards give you the details.

Entry to the site costs 20/−.

Access

Car Olorgasailie Prehistoric Site lies 1.5 km to the east of the C58 Nairobi − Magadi road, about 60 km south-west of Nairobi. The road is tarred all the way to Magadi. The site is well signposted.

Bus/Hitch There is one bus each way per day between Nairobi and Magadi via Olorgasailie. From Nairobi matatus run out to Kiserian or occasionally as far as Olepolos, beyond the southern flank of the Ngong Hills, and hitching from there is possible with patience.

CAMPING

Olorgasailie is very hot, and no place to rush around, so it's worth staying a night here to see the sites in the cool of the evening or morning. The view over the ancient lake-bed towards the cliffs and distant mountains still has a prehistoric feel.

The campsite is on a small grassy area above the digs. A large tree provides shade, or you can use the tables and benches in the picnic shelter. A few basic but clean bandas are also available for hire.

Cost 20/− ppn.
Facilities Water from a borehole, toilets, bucket shower, storage hut (bring your own padlock), fireplace, table and benches. Lamp hire 10/−. No duka nearby, bring everything you need.
Security The site is fenced, but problems are very unlikely.
Bandas 50/− double.

45 km beyond Olorgasailie the tarred road ends at **Lake Magadi** a huge soda lake just 30 km north of the Tanzanian border. It's even hotter here than at Olorgasailie, and the lake shimmers pink and white in the sun. ICI have built a large factory and workers' town with a petrol station, a market and a few dukas. It's possible to camp on the outskirts of the town, near the golf course(!). If you have your own vehicle you can travel south towards Mount Shompole and Lake Natron, or cross the lake on a narrow causeway and head west towards the Ewaso Ngiro River and the Nguruman Escarpment. Climbing away from the lake it gets cooler and there are many places to camp, especially along the river. To travel here, though, it's essential to be completely self-contained.

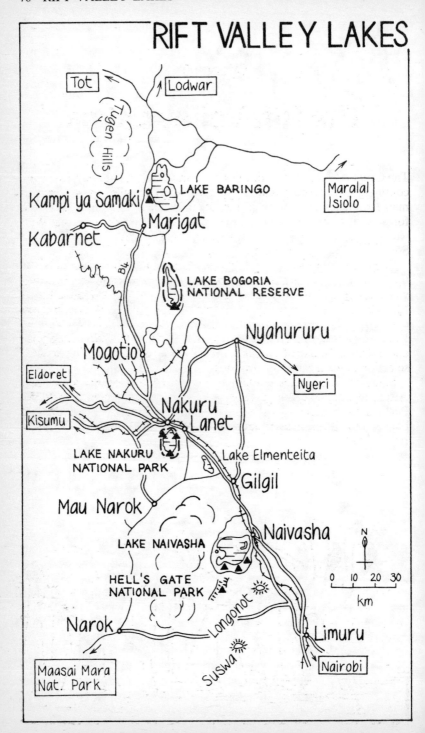

Chapter 9

The Rift Valley Lakes

The Great African Rift Valley lies like a huge trench half-way across the continent from Mozambique to the Red Sea. The valley passes through many countries and a wide variety of landscapes, from desert to fertile forest and farmland. On the valley floor are a number of lakes, their waters trapped between the steep escarpments on either side of the rift. Some of these lakes are among the largest in Africa.

The eastern branch of the Rift Valley cuts through Kenya, entering the country in the south near Lake Magadi and leaving in the north where the waters of Lake Turkana cross into Sudan and Ethiopia. Lakes Magadi and Turkana lie at the extreme ends of the country, and are covered in the Maasailand and North chapters, but in the centre of Kenya is a line of smaller lakes, Naivasha, Elmenteita, Nakuru, Bogoria and Baringo, most of which are easily accessible and offer a wide selection of ideal camping locations.

Some of these lakes contain fresh water while others are saline. Attractions include hot springs, geysers and a profusion of wildlife. Particularly famous are the huge flocks of flamingos that migrate between the lakes on an irregular basis as the water levels mysteriously rise and fall.

LAKE NAIVASHA

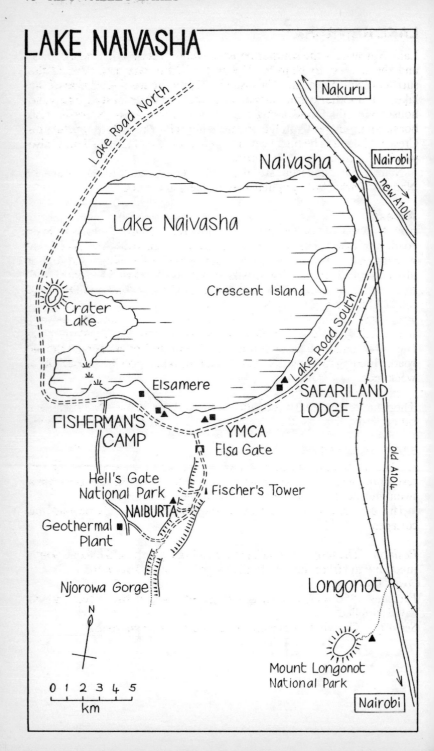

LAKE NAIVASHA

Lake Naivasha is the southernmost of Kenya's central rift valley lakes, and the nearest to Nairobi. The water in the lake is fresh and the surrounding land fertile. Naivasha town, on the north-east side of the lake, was a settler community and a number of colonial style farms and houses are still found along the lakeside road. Lake Naivasha also boasts an up-market hotel, a private sailing club, and a bird sanctury on Crescent Island. The bird-watching here is excellent and the lake is also popular for fishing and windsurfing.

Near Lake Naivasha are the Hell's Gate and Mount Longanot National Parks, both popular with walkers and campers.

Access

car   Naivasha town lies just off the new A104 Nairobi – Nakuru main road. The lake is south-west of the town and encircled by Lake Road which meets the old A104 5 km south of Naivasha. From Nairobi it is also possible to approach Naivasha on the old A104 via Longanot. Both main roads are tarred but Lake Road South is in bad condition and impassable after heavy rain.

Bus/Hitch   Buses and matatus run regularly along both the old and new roads between Nairobi and Naivasha, and less regularly from Naivasha round the Lake South road. To reach Longanot take the old road. Hitching to Naivasha, and round the lake, is possible, especially at weekends.

There are three campsites on the southern shore of Lake Naivasha, and others at the Hell's Gate and Longonot National Parks.

SAFARILAND LODGE

A lakeside 'tourist village' overlooking the lake with a central bar and restaurant, and cottages among the trees in the grounds. The lodge has a swimming pool, and horse-riding and boats are available.

The campsite is at one side of the pleasant grounds beyond the cottages.

Position   The lodge entrance gate is 10 km from the Lake Road South junction, and from the gate to the lodge is another kilometre.
Cost   100/- ppn.
Facilities   Showers, toilets, drinking water, open fire places but no wood supplied.
Security   The whole lodge area is fenced and well guarded.

YMCA

The YMCA is also called the Youth Hostel, although its official status is currently under review, probably because it is very rundown, with ramshackle bandas, an empty shop, and frequent problems with the water supply making showers unusable and toilets very unpleasant. The campsite is in a shady field, with a hippo grazing ground and the muddy shore of the lake a short walk away.

Position   The YMCA is 16 km from the Lake Road junction, on the lake side of the road. Look for the red triangle sign.

Cost   20/− ppn to camp.

Facilities   Showers and toilets (see above). Firewood 4/−. The nearest shop at the Sulmac factory workers' village 2 km further along Lake Road South.

Bandas   30/− ppn.

FISHERMAN'S CAMP

At the entrance to Fisherman's Camp is a Youth Hostel sign. This causes confusion with the YMCA only 4 km away, and is something of a misnomer as hostel facilities are only in operation between April and October. However, Fisherman's Camp is a pleasant collection of bandas (190/-) and campsite (tent hire 40/-, firewood 20/-) in a grassy, shaded area close to the lake.

Rowing boats can be taken on the lake free of charge, and fishing rods can be hired. This is a pleasant way to spend the afternoon or evening, but do not ignore the warning notices about lake conditions and the danger of hippos.

Position   Fisherman's Camp is 20 km from the Lake Road junction.

Cost   30/− ppn for camping.

Facilities   Water, toilets, firewood. The nearest shops are at the Sulmac village.

HELL'S GATE NATIONAL PARK

South of Lake Naivasha is Hell's Gate National Park, popular with walkers and campers who can enter without a vehicle and move noislessly past herds of zebra and gazelle. The park is flanked by imposing sheer cliffs which lead to a narrow canyon containing hot springs and geysers. In the park is Ol Ndumbai Public Campsite with excellent views. Standard park fees are payable.

Position   The Elsa Gate entrance to the park is signposted on the left 16.5 km from the Lake Road junction, just past the YMCA. From here to the gate is a further 2 km.

MOUNT LONGONOT NATIONAL PARK

This park is 20km south of Naivasha town, near the small centre of the same name. A car is not required (or usable). Walkers can climb up to the rim of the text-book style extinct volcano and make a dramatic circuit of the crater. The campsite, with water and toilets, is at the park gate. Standard park fees are payable.

Fischer's Tower, Hell's Gate National Park.

LAKE NAKURU NATIONAL PARK

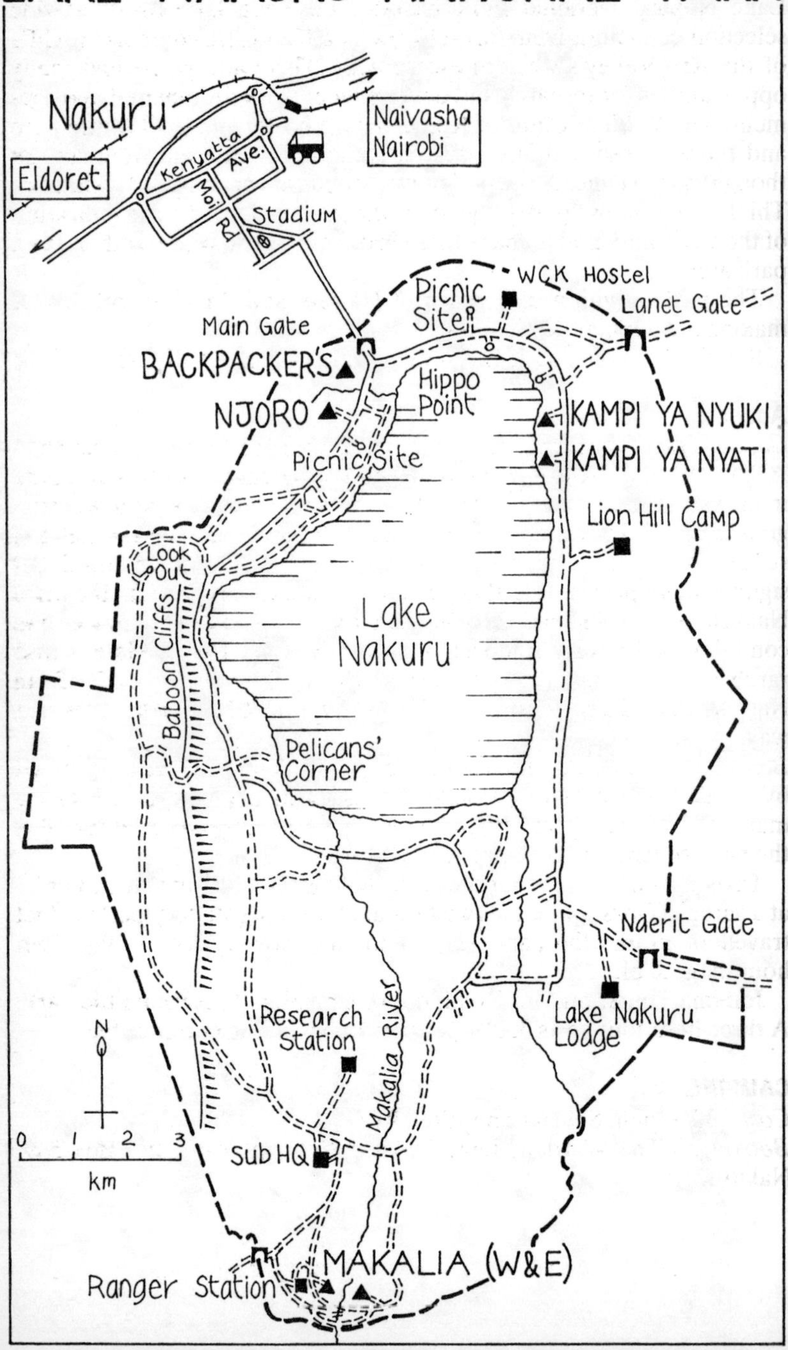

Nakuru

Eldoret

Kenyatta Ave.

Moi Rd.

Naivasha
Nairobi

Stadium

WCK Hostel
Lanet Gate

Picnic Site

Main Gate

BACKPACKER'S

NJORO

Picnic Site

Hippo Point

KAMPI YA NYUKI

KAMPI YA NYATI

Lion Hill Camp

Look Out

Baboon Cliffs

Lake Nakuru

Pelicans' Corner

Naderit Gate

Research Station

Makalia River

Lake Nakuru Lodge

Sub HQ

N

0 1 2 3
km

Ranger Station

MAKALIA (W&E)

LAKE NAKURU NATIONAL PARK

Lake Nakuru National Park includes the soda lake itself, a wide selection of habitats from forest to grassland, and also contains the cliffs of the Rift Valley's western escarpment. This variety provides many opportunities for research and development of environmental management; The Wildlife Clubs of Kenya have a hostel and field centre here and there is also a rhino research station. Wildlife and tourism are thoughtfully balanced, the park is well organised and in good condition. This lushness is also partly due to the absence of elephants: an indication of the environmental damage these browsers can do when confined to a park area.

The park is within easy reach of Nairobi and drivable with 2WD, making it a popular destination.

Standard national park entrance fees are payable at all gates.

Access

Car Nakuru town is about 150 km north-west of Nairobi on the main A104 road (tar). The most commonly used route into the park is via the main gate, 4 km south of Nakuru town centre. From Kenyatta Avenue, go down Moi Rd, fork left into Stadium Rd, and continue through the suburbs to the park boundary and main gate. This route is tarred and signposted in places. It is also possible to enter the park from the main Nakuru − Nairobi road through Lanet Gate. This dirt road is in bad condition and poorly signposted, so rarely used. Nderit Gate is also rarely used although some private cars and tourist vehicles coming from Naivasha or Maasai Mara via Mau Narok and Elmenteita enter this way.

Bus/Hitch Nakuru is the fourth largest town in Kenya and well served by public transport. It's possible to walk from the town centre to the main gate, where you can try hitching a ride. Walking is not permitted in the park beyond the Backpacker's Campsite.

Taxis can be hired to tour the park. Ask outside the railway station or at a garage. Taxis sometimes wait beside the main gate to chauffeur foot travellers around the park. Expect to pay between 200 − 300/− per hour, negotiable.

Jomima Tours, on Moi Road, operate minibus trips round the park. A three hour tour costs 350/− per person, including entrance fee.

CAMPING

Cost 30/− ppn. Special campsites 300/− psw.
Bookings The Warden, Lake Nakuru National Park, PO Box 539, Nakuru.

Backpacker's Campsite

Just inside main gate, and too close to be secluded. The park rangers allow people without vehicles to wait for lifts here. Monkeys are also used to tourists and can be a real nuisance. Keep an eye on your food and gear.

Facilities Pit-toilets, basic showers, water (supply not always reliable).

Njoro Campsite

Only 1 km from the gate, but set back off the main track amongst trees. Its pleasant roomy setting and easy access makes it popular with safari companies.

Facilities Water tap, pit toilets. Firewood for sale. Heed the notices asking 'Please use the toilets not the bush'.

Makalia Campsites

Two sites on either side of the Makalia Falls at the southern end of the park. Far from the lake, so less frequently used by tourists, although visits from buffalo and gazelle, on their way to drink at the river, are possible.

Facilities Grass and shade are plentiful. Pit toilets leave the bush for the wildlife. Firewood can be collected from the Falls.

In the East Campsite the supply from the tank to the tap and shower cannot be relied upon, so bring water, or use the river. The water supply in the West Campsite is likely to be more reliable as there is a rangers station on the bluff above the site.

Kampi Ya Nyuki Special Campsite

In the north-east part of the park, a grassy lake-side clearing beneath yellow-barked acacia trees. The site is often used by the more up-market safari companies.

Facilities none.

Kampi Ya Nyati Special Campsite

Near Kampi Ya Nyuki and similar, although slightly smaller.

We camped for a night at Makalia Falls, right at the southern end of the park. It was beautiful. We had the whole place to ourselves. It seems the campsite is rarely used. The water tank in the East campsite is empty, but this is a small price to pay for solitude in an unspoilt campsite. The animals are unused to campers here too, I think. The old buffalo who wandered past, just a few hundred metres from the site, was as surprised to see us as we were surprised to see him. We both retreated in a suitably dignified manner. (Richard Lewis, Britain)

LAKE BOGORIA NATIONAL RESERVE

Lake Bogoria is a saline lake, lying in a scorched, rocky landscape with hot springs and exploding geysers along the western shore and the steep dark wall of the Laikipa Escarpment towering over its eastern side. First impressions are of a harsh and lifeless environment but the lake sides are usually dotted pink with flocks of flamingos and the park does contain some herds of gazelle and antelope, including the rare greater kudu.

The northern part of the reserve is popular with visitors. Near the hot springs is a picnic site, which is sometimes crowded at weekends. The area south of the hot springs is less frequently visited as the roads are very rocky and steep.

Standard national reserve entrance fees are payable at all gates.

Access

Car   Lake Bogoria is about 60 km directly north of Nakuru. The most commonly used route into the park is via Loboi Gate in the north of the reserve. From Nakuru take the main B4 road (tarred) north towards Marigat. 4 km south of Marigat turn east to Loboi on the E461 dirt road. This junction is signposted. Loboi Gate is reached after 21 km.

It is also possible to enter the reserve via Majimoto Gate, 18 km south of Loboi Gate. To reach this gate turn east off the B4 at Mogotio and follow dirt roads through sisal estates for 24 km to Mugurin. Continue on the main track and turn right after about 20 km to Majimoto Gate. On this route it is also possible to enter via Emsos Gate, at the southern end of the park. Follow the above directions to Mugurin. After 1 km fork right off the dirt road onto a poor track. From Mugurin to Emsos Gate is 14 km dropping steeply for final 3 km. Leaving the reserve this way, high clearance and 4WD are essential.

An alternative approach to Mugurin runs from Subukia, on the B5 Nyahururu − Nakuru road, via Kisinana. This involves over 60 km of dirt road driving, and, although passable, this route is rarely used by tourists.

Bus/Hitch   Buses and matatus between Nakuru and Marigat run regularly along the main B4. One bus goes via Mugurin and Loboi each day in each direction. Times are not fixed. A matatu serves the sisal estate centres, but again schedules are vague.

Even in the absence of predatory animals pedestrian access to the reserve is forbidden. It may be possible to hitch at the Loboi Gate road junction (4 km south of Marigat) or at the gate itself, although this is a less visited park so you may have to wait a long time. Coming from Mugurin the chances of a lift are even slighter. Without a car this route, and especially the approach via Kisinana, is only for the most hardened walkers (or mountain bikers). Even if you do hike to Emsos Gate, and are allowed into the reserve, leaving by one of the other gates still involves a long, hot walk with no water on the way. The hot springs picnic site is the first probable place to pick up a lift to Loboi, and you may have some explaining to do to the rangers if you exit this way.

LAKE BOGORIA NATIONAL RESERVE

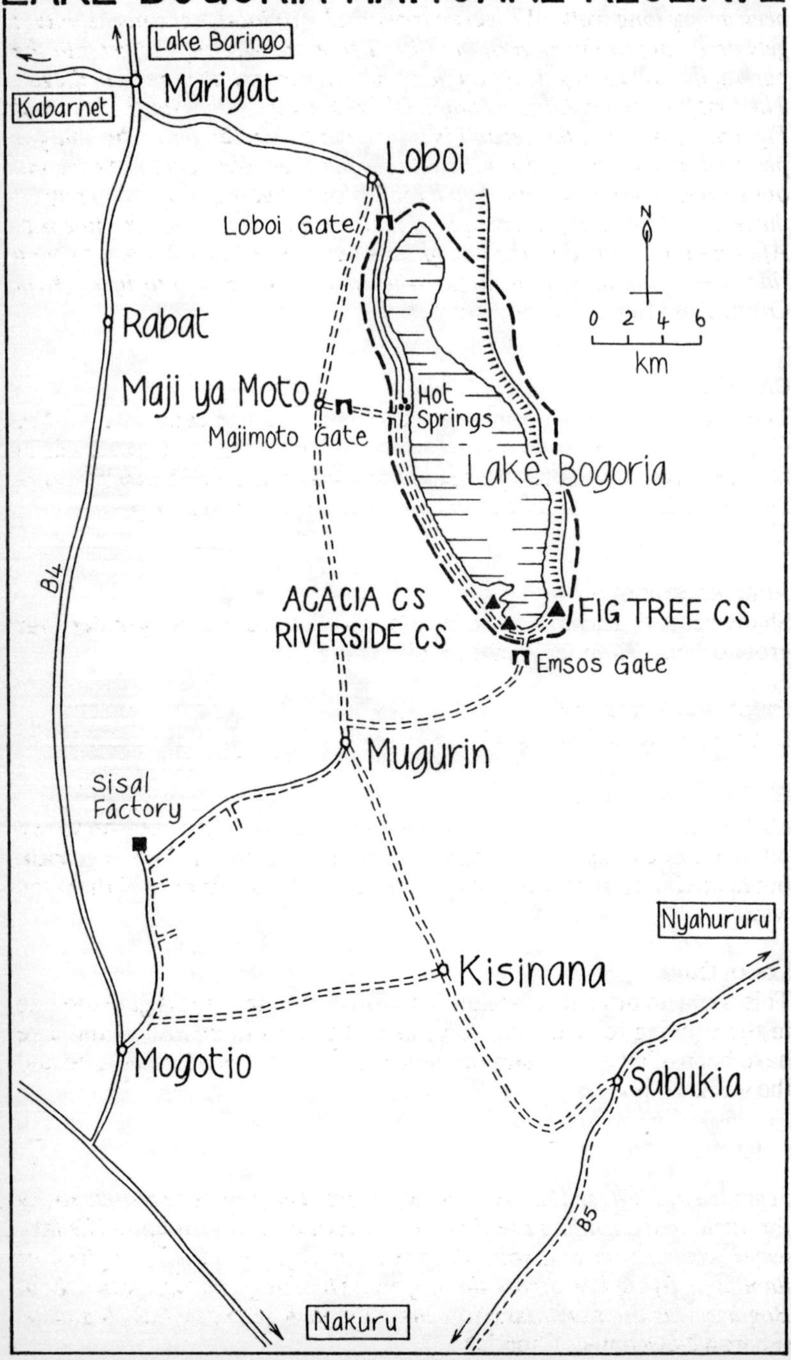

Kabarnet

Lake Baringo

Marigat

Loboi

Loboi Gate

Rabat

Maji ya Moto

Majimoto Gate

Hot Springs

Lake Bogoria

N

0 2 4 6
km

B4

ACACIA CS
RIVERSIDE CS

FIG TREE CS

Emsos Gate

Mugurin

Sisal Factory

Nyahururu

Kisinana

Mogotio

Sabukia

B5

Nakuru

We had been told it was possible to walk to Lake Bogoria from the Nakuru Road. It probably is, but I'm glad we got a lift. It would have been a very long walk. We were carrying a lot of food in the packs, and it gets pretty hot in this part of the Rift. There are two ways to get into the park at the southern gate if you don't have a car, and they're both illegal. The first is to avoid the gate completely and head straight for the lake and Fig Tree Campsite, the second is to ask the lonely ranger at the gate for permission to walk into the park as far as Fig Tree. We went for the second option and got in OK, although it took a lot of talking. We had to pay all the fees, but camped for a couple of nights at Fig Tree which is a fine site. After that we walked to the hot springs picnic site and managed to get a ride with some tourists in a car who took us back to Marigat. (Arik Orbach and Limor Rozen, Israel)

CAMPING

The reserve has three campsites, all at the southern end of the lake. Campers need to be completely self-sufficient as the sites are all in remote positions with very limited facilities. There is no other accommodation in the reserve. Security problems are very unlikely.
Cost   20/− ppn.

Acacia Campsite

Shady beneath acacia trees on the lake shore, but quite stony under your groundsheet. Pit toilet in bad condition.

Riverside Campsite

Shady site. No facilities and no river!

Fig Tree Campsite

Massive fig trees give shade, a stream provides water, and broken down pit toilets encourage bush latrines. Upstream is a natural bubbling bath, but upstream further still a village extracts water and inputs all the usual waste.

Loboi Gate

This is not an official campsite, but visitors arriving at this gate too late in the evening to reach the campsites at the southern end of the lake have been allowed to camp on the patch of grass between the gate and the workers' houses.

I camped at Fig Tree Campsite for one night. The ground was quite rocky for pitching the tent but the view in the morning was beautiful. The lake water was smooth and still, shattered only by the occasional flock of flamingos flying low across the surface. The thing that struck me about Bogoria was the quietness. Somehow the heat seems to kill all sound. (Sharon Newcombe, Canada)

LAKE BARINGO

Lake Baringo is a freshwater lake, northernmost of the central Rift Valley Lakes. The surrounding land is home to the Njemps tribe, while crocodiles, hippos and over 450 species of birds live in and around the lake.

Lake Baringo's scenery and easy access make it a popular tourist destination. Accommodation includes an exclusive 'club' hotel on the lake-shore, another on an island in the centre of the lake, and a campsite.

Access

Car   Lake Baringo's main settlement is Kampi Ya Samaki, a fishing town on the western shore of the lake, about 120 km north of Nakuru. From Nakuru drive north on the main B4 road, through Marigat, and turn east for Kampi Ya Samaki 123 km after Nakuru. The road is tarred all the way to this junction and as far north as Loruk. From the junction to Kampi Ya Samaki is about 3 km.

Bus/Hitch   Buses and matatus run from Nakuru to Marigat and from there to Kampi Ya Samaki. Traffic is frequent from Nakuru as far as Marigat, but less so beyond Marigat. Other routes involve more patience.

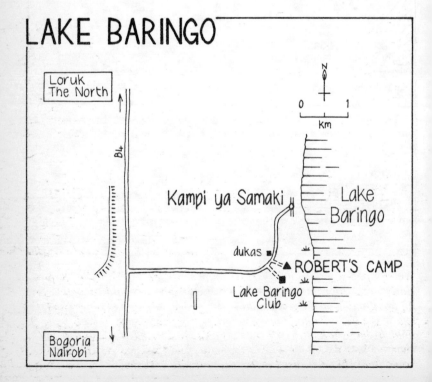

ROBERT'S CAMP

Robert's Camp is about 2 km south of Kampi Ya Samaki, on the west shore of the lake. Long established under shady acacia trees, the camp is beautiful and easily accessible, making it a favourite with independent tourists and with some of the camping safari companies. Bandas are also available.

Position   Robert's Camp is 1 km from the junction of the main B4 and the Kampi Ya Samaki road.
Cost   40/– ppn.
Facilities   Clean showers, water and firewood. Basic supplies available at the *dukas* opposite the campsite entrance, or in Kampi Ya Samaki.
Security   Fence and askari.
Bandas   160/– double.

Day membership (50/-) at the **Lake Baringo Club** allows non-residents to use the facilities (including the pool) and may be redeemed if you have a meal. The club also runs morning and evening bird walks led by an expert ornithologist.

A small boat serves **Ol Kokwe Island** allowing exploration of hot springs and flamingo-filled crater lake.

We stopped a night at Robert's Camp with Special Camping Safaris. Early in the morning we went down to the lake side and saw a herd of hippos grazing on the grass at the water's edge: huge grey lumps with little legs at the bottom and little ears at the top. We watched them for a while until a giant goliath heron landed nearby scaring them and they all charged into the water with a tremendous splash and noise. Strange, you'd think they'd be used to the local birdlife. (Louise Harvey, USA)

WEST OF THE RIFT

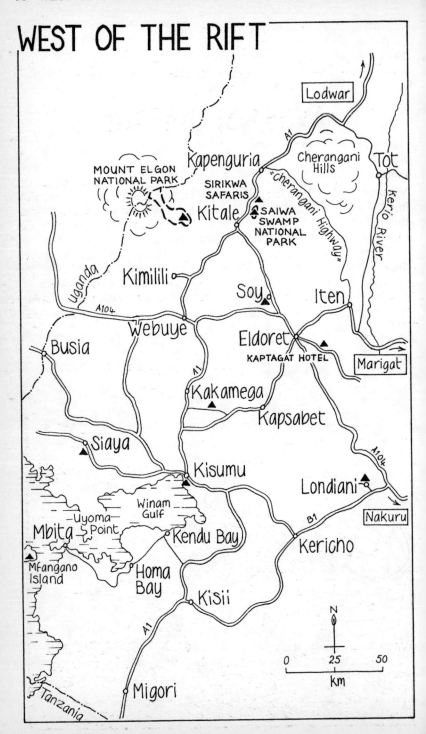

Chapter 10

West of the Rift

Official campsites are few in this tourist backwater around Lake Victoria. There are no big game parks, no high mountains, and no palm lined golden sand beaches to attract Kenya's short-stay visitors, and therefore accommodation is limited to occasional classy hotels, basic local B&L's and to enterprise camping.

When you have tired of the tourist routes go west for a less frantic, more friendly experience. A place to relax, where you will not get charged extra, and someone always has time for a mid-day chat out of the sun. The only hassle you may encounter here is from the kids calling out *"mzungu"*, as white faces are a comparative rarity in some rural places.

KISUMU

Kisumu, the third largest town in Kenya, is in the far west of the country on the eastern shore of Lake Victoria. The town was established in colonial times at the end of the railway line from the coast as a port for the ships running between Kenya and Uganda (and later Tanzania) on Lake Victoria. When the East African Community disbanded in 1977 Kisumu lost much of its commercial significance and the town fell on hard times. This air of stagnation is still apparent, but Kisumu is not an unpleasant town, well worth a visit on its own account and as a focus for wider travels around western Kenya.

There are hotels for all budgets in Kisumu, plenty of shops, an excellent market and a British Council library.

Access

Car   Kisumu is about 350 km north-west of Nairobi. The most direct route by car from Nairobi follows the main A104 through Nakuru to Mau Summit, then takes the B1 through Kericho to Kisumu. The roads are tarred all the way.

Bus/Hitch   Fast buses rush between Nairobi and Kisumu, some overnight, as well as the usual slower country buses and matatus. The daily or nightly train between Nairobi and Kisumu is a more relaxed form of public transport. For second class seats booking is advisable.

Hitching on these busy roads is no problem. You should be able to do Nairobi — Kisumu in a day.

Kisumu town has two campsites.

DUNGA RESTAURANT AND CAMPING

Dunga Restaurant is at Hippo Point, a popular spot for evening and weekend visitors, ideally sited for views of Lake Victoria and nightly sunsets. The campsite is a field at the side of the restaurant and as yet is little used.

Position   Hippo Point is on the lake shore about 4 km south of Kisumu town centre. The road to Dunga Restaurant and Campsite winds through suburbs and shambas and is well signposted, but the distances are a little optimistic. No bus runs out this way.

Cost   50/-

Facilities   The flush toilet and showers also serve the restaurant customers. No shop. Food at the restaurant ranges from snacks at 30/- to meals at 120/-.

Security   The car park and campsite is inside a compound, patrolled by an askari.

YWCA

The YWCA hostel is used mainly by Kenyan students and school groups, although foreign visitors are welcome. The campsite is a grassy area beside the hostel. It is not secluded but can be easily reached by backpackers.

Position   The YWCA is in the centre of Kisumu opposite a small grassy area near the market and bus station.

Cost   20/– ppn.

Facilities   Toilet and showers in the hostel. Meals available in the hostel. Shops and market nearby.

Security   Fence and askari.

Bed in hostel   35/–.

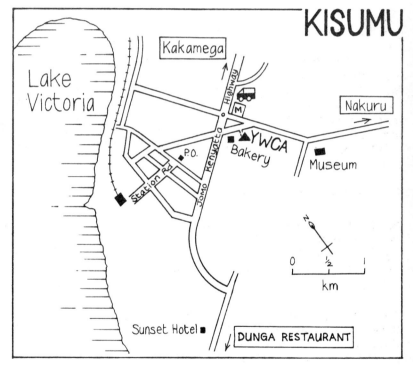

Kisumu town is at the head of **The Winam Gulf**, a large inlet which divides the province of Nyanza into its northern and southern parts. Large steamers and smaller wooden ferry-boats with out-board motors cross the gulf at various points. A regular ferry runs between Mbita and Uyoma Point which makes a complete circular tour of the gulf possible. Interesting diversions include **Rusinga Island**, joined to the mainland by a causeway at Mbita, and **Mfangano Island**, a more serious proposition involving a long steamer or boat ride from Mbita. The south Nyanza district has no official campsites, but in the past campers have been allowed to pitch their tents at schools and police stations.

When we were travelling around the South Nyanza district, we decided to catch the boat over to Mfangano Island. We'd heard vague rumours about ancient cave paintings hidden somewhere on the island, but our main reason for visiting was, quite simply, because it was there.

A narrow wooden ferry-boat runs from Mbita to Mfangano every day, leaving in the early morning, packed with passengers and produce. There's also a more comfortable but less frequent steamer service between Mbita and Mfangano, which calls at Sena, the main town on the island. The small daily boat stops at Sena and a number of other places along Mfangano's northern shoreline. We stayed on the boat to Wakola, the end of the line, and nearest to the mysterious caves.

Mfangano has no roads or vehicles of any sort but the island is criss-crossed by paths and tracks joining the numerous small settlements along the shoreline and on the central high ground. The island makes an ideal place to explore for a couple of days, providing some interesting backpacking country. Accommodation is limited to a single government rest house at Sena, so a tent has obvious advantages.

The numerous paths make a guide worthwhile too. Even though visitors to Mfangano are few, the locals are not completely unused to foreigners, and a guide should not be too difficult to find. We arranged a guide in Wakola to show us the cave paintings. These were very faint, and probably only of real interest to specialists; the walk from Wakola up to the caves, though, was excellent, through forest and shambas to open bush on the highest part of the island with good views over Lake Victoria and the surrounding islands.

We asked permission to camp in a compound belonging to a local family, but were offered an empty hut instead, so we unrolled our sleeping bags onto the dry earth floor. We were also cooked a meal as part of the deal. It seems the locals have done this kind of thing before and are happy to have the chance to earn an extra 100/– or so catering for visiting campers or hikers. If staying with a family on the island expect to pay what you'd pay in a B&L or hoteli. If you want to provide for yourself, note that supplies on Mfangano are limited. Sena and Wakula have very basic dukas and hotelis, but it's best to take all you need from Mbita.

A good 'itinerary' for campers visiting Mfangano might be to take a small boat to Wakola, visit the caves and stay the night, then walk to Sena with or without a guide, camping where you like (with permission if necessary) depending upon your time limits, and catch a boat or steamer back to the mainland.   (D.E., J.B.)

LONDIANI

Londiani is a small town at the northern end of the Mau massif, just north of the main road between Kisumu and Nakuru. The area was settled by farmers during the colonial times and was particularly famous for its lamb. More recently many of the big farms have been divided in land redistribution schemes so shambas and small-holdings now cover much of the area.

On some maps a number of forests are indicated in the Londiani area, but much of the land is taken by conifer plantations. Shaved hillsides are an increasingly common sight as the land is cleared and planted. The only remaining patch of indigenous forest in this region is to the north-east of Londiani town itself. This has been declared a forest reserve, to protect it from clearing or re-planting, and a forestry research centre has been established. Nearby is a forestry college, a saw-mill and, somewhat surprisingly, a campsite, some bandas and a brand new guest house.

The campsite was originally established here as the forest was popular with hikers and bird-watchers. According to the warden the number of campers using the site has dropped in recent years, although the site remains open.

Access
Car Londiani town lies 3 km north-west of the main B1 Kisumu – Mau Summit road (tarred). The C35 dirt road to Londiani leaves the B1 at a junction about 12 km west of Mau Summit.

Bus/Hitch Plenty of buses and matatus run beween Kisumu or Kericho and Nakuru or Mau Summit. Ask to get off at the Londiani junction. Hitching on the main road is no problem. Matatus run to Londiani town but the road to the campsite is less than 2 km from the junction.

Note that Mount Loldiani is spelt Londiani on some maps.

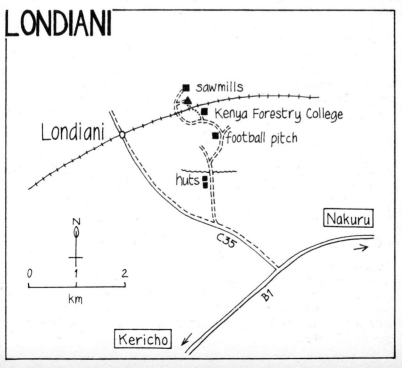

CAMPING

Visitors should report to the principal of the college, and will then be
shown the campsite which is in a field near the college social club.
Forest rangers and other people in the nearby workers' compound mean
that the site is not secluded.

Position From the B1 follow the C35 for about 1.7 km, and before
reaching the town turn right at a sign to 'Ministry of Environment and
Natural Resources, Forestry Dept., District Forest Office'. Pass some
huts and shambas, cross a small river, fork right, then left round a
football field to reach the Forestry College buildings after about
2 km.
Cost 5/– ppn.
Facilities Water, toilets in the club house.
Security Fence and askaris.
Bandas 40/– ppn. Guest House: 100/– single, 150/– double.
Bookings (not necessary for camping) The Principal, Kenya Forestry
College, PO Box 8, Londiani.

SIAYA

Although Siaya is the capital of Siaya district, it is a small quiet town with a pleasant atmosphere. The white houses, lack of large trees, and fields of crops growing right up to the road give it a vaguely Spanish feel. The town is higher than Kisumu and always noticeably less humid.

Siaya is a convenient stopping point for people travelling to or from Uganda, or makes a good base for a circular tour of the Winam Gulf to take in Kisumu, Kisii, the eastern shore of Lake Victoria, and the Mbita − Uyoma ferry.

Siaya has a market, a hotel, some basic B&Ls, and a campsite 2 km out of town.

Access

Car   Siaya town lies 10 km south of the main B1 Kisumu − Busia road about 60 km north-west of Kisumu. The C27/C28 road, which forks from the B1 at Kisian and runs via Ndori and Siaya to Ebusonga, has also been tarred recently and is now the most direct route to Siaya.

Bus/Hitch   Buses and matatus run regularly to Siaya from Kisumu. Hitching is possible, but private vehicles are rare on the roads in this area.

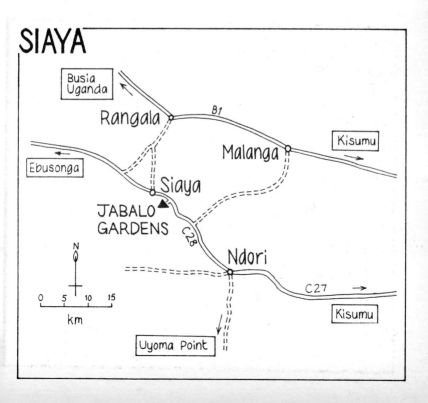

JABALO GARDENS

Jabalo Gardens is a group of cottages, a restaurant, and a campsite set in a large garden, much of which is still cultivated. Tents can be pitched on the neat lawn. The whole site is simple and quiet.

Position   Jabalo Gardens is 2 km east of Siaya on the tarred road in from Kisumu.
Cost   20/− ppn.
Facilities   Clean pit toilet, water, bucket shower cubicle, firewood. Restaurant (meals between 15 − 35/−), bar, lounge, secluded outdoor patio with garden chairs. Dukas nearby.
Security   Fence and askari. No trouble ever reported.
Cottages/bandas   50/− ppn (including breakfast).
Address   PO Box 189, Siaya. Tel: Siaya 115.

Information supplied by Sabine Tamm, Canada.

I camped at Jabalo Gardens not long after it opened. It's a really nice place, secluded and quiet, right off the beaten track. The sheer number of people in western Kenya can get to you sometimes, and this is a good place to escape for a while. The lady who runs Jabalo Gardens is genuinely friendly and likes to meet visitors. Fresh bread and eggs are available. Bananas, oranges, spices and vegetables grow in the garden and most of the food in the restaurant comes fresh from the garden; great for vegetarians! The cook told me that with warning he can also prepare a variety of dishes; Indian or European food, or even the local Luo speciality, cooked blood meal. Not so good for vegetarians! (Sabine Tamm, Canada)

KAKAMEGA FOREST

Kakamega Forest is a tiny remnant of the equatorial rainforest which once stretched across southern and western Kenya, an extension of the great forests of the Zaire basin and Central Africa. Kakamega Forest lies to the south-east of Kakamega town, and is currently classed as a forest reserve although plans exist to declare the forest a full national reserve.

The forest is an isolated haven for the many unique animals and birds associated with the fast disappearing indigenous trees and plants. The great blue touraco is the star attraction amongst the birds, and the possibility of a glimpse of the rare De Brazza monkey, or a night viewing of a bushbaby or potto adds to the interest.

The only place to stay is the Rest House at the forest station on the western edge of the forest near the village of Shinyalu, 15 km south-east of Kakamega town. Camping is permitted here.

Access

Car   Kakamega town is about 50 km north of Kisumu on the main A1 Kisumu – The North road (tarred). At Khayega turn east off the A1 and follow the good dirt road for 7 km to Shinyalu. Ignore the left fork in Shinyalu and follow the dirt road eastwards through Virhombe towards Tindinya and the main Kisumu – Eldoret road. After 5 km turn left (north) onto a small track to the forest station. On the Survey of Kenya Route Map the forest station is marked.

Bus/Hitch   Buses and matatus run regularly between Kisumu and Kakamega town. Get off the bus at Khayega. Matatus run from here to Shinyalu or on to Tindinya, on the main Kisumu – Eldoret road, via the forest station junction. The 12 km walk from Khayega to the forest station junction passes through farmland and shambas. One bus runs every day in each direction between Kisumu and Eldoret via Shinyalu and the forest station junction. This bus leaves either destination in the early morning and passes the junction mid-morning. Ask to be dropped at the forest station (sometimes called simply 'Forest'), near the Isecheno Primary School.

Alternatively, take the Kisumu – Eldoret bus as far as Tindinya (marked on some maps as Chepsonoi), 21 km from Kapsabet. Signposted 'Kisieni; 12 km D267'. Matatus from this junction run towards Shinyalu (sometimes called Osore) via the Rest house.

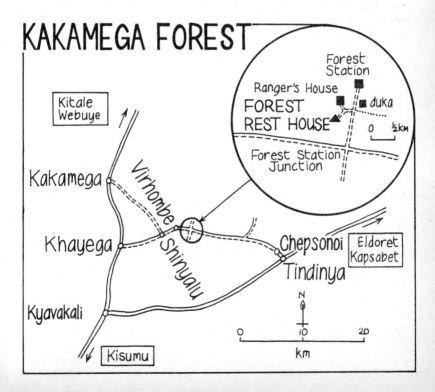

CAMPING

The Forest Rest House is small and basic, with only four double rooms, no electricity and an erratic water supply. But this is part of its charm. Constructed on wooden stilts, the verandah overlooks the seemingly solid mass of the forest, almost as if the rest house itself is built up in the trees. A small lawn behind the rest house provides the camping area.

Position   After leaving the main dirt road at the forest station junction, follow the dirt track towards the forest station (signposted). After 300 m turn left again to the rest house.

Cost   5/− ppn for camping.

Facilities   Pit toilet, bucket shower. Water often has to be collected from the nearby wardens' house (used in the film *Kitchen Toto*). Guided birdwalks can be arranged, and kerosene lamps can be hired. The nearby duka is rumoured to sell chai, and meals by arrangement, but keeps unfathomable hours. Dukas and hotelis keeping more reliable hours are 2 km towards Shinyalu at Virhombe.

Security   An askari at night, but no security problems have been reported.

Rest House   Bed in double room, 30/− ppn.

Bookings/Enquiries   The Forester, Kakamega Forest Station, PO Box 88, Kakamega.

We camped at Kakamega Forest Resthouse during the rainy season and retreated to the shelter of the verandah during the evening downpour.

Next morning as the sun came out and the forest began to steam we went for a walk in the forest. Leonard, the caretaker, and Jackson, a forest ranger, both organise walks and it's well worth going with one them if you can. There's a bit of competition between these two, the money they earn from visitors tops up their meagre wages (agree on a fee before going — about 30/− per person), but they are both very knowledgeable and interesting. They know all about the birds and animals in the forest and Jackson also has a great deal to say about the trees and bushes. He can tell you the names in English, Kiswahili and his own tribal language and understands their medicinal properties and traditional significance. I was suffering from a sore throat and my coughing was frightening the birds. Jackson pulled out the root of one of the bushes in the forest and told me to suck it. Half an hour later my throat was cured.

After we'd paid Jackson for the walk he obviously decided he'd earned himself a pombe or two and came back to see us in the evening a little the worse for drink. As if the English and Kiswahili terminology hadn't been enough that morning, he insisted on telling us again the names of all the trees we'd seen. Only this time, he managed to produce all their Latin scientific names! (D.E., J.B.)

ELDORET AND AREA

Eldoret is a thriving market town and business centre, on the main road from Nakuru to Webuye and the Ugandan border, about 300 km north west of Nairobi. Most visitors pass through Eldoret on their way to Uganda or the north, and Eldoret is a good place to stock up on all sorts of supplies. Eldoret has a large number of basic B&Ls, some mid-range hotels and, on the north-east side of town, the impressive new Sirikwa Hotel.

Access

Car   Eldoret is on the main A104 Nairobi – Uganda road about 150 km north of Nakuru and 120 km west of the Malaba border crossing. These routes, and others from Kitale to the north and Kapsabet to the south, are tarred.

Bus/Hitch   Eldoret is a major centre and is served by buses and matatus from other towns in the area and from Nairobi. Passenger trains run between Malaba and Nairobi via Eldoret two or three times a week. Hitchers heading in any direction on the tarred roads will find plenty of traffic.

Until 1988 the only campsite in Eldoret was the Wagon Wheels Hotel. This hotel is currently undergoing extensive renovation, and it is uncertain if the hotel will continue to accept campers after re-opening.

The Kaptagat Hotel, 23 km east of Eldoret on the C54 (tarred as far as the Nyaru crossroads), is another place which used to allow camping, but this old colonial style country club is also currently closed 'for renovation'. If the hotel does re-open, and is modernised, it will be a pleasant place to camp. A group of bungalows with verandahs are set in a semi-circle around a large garden with flower beds and decorative shrubs. The camping site is on one side of this lawn.

SOY COUNTRY CLUB

Soy Country Club, 25 km north of Eldoret, is how the Kaptagat Hotel would have looked. Soy has managed to survive the passing of colonial days and weekend visits are still popular with Kenyans and expats, although the staff seem unused to campers. Bungalows surround a grassy quadrangle with manicured flower beds and neat paths. Beyond the bungalows is a large lawn for camping.

Position   From Eldoret take A104 road towards Uganda. After 15 km turn right (north), and take the B2 towards Kitale. The Club (sign-posted) is on the left after 10 km, just before Soy centre. Buses and matatus run between Eldoret and Kitale via Soy. Hitchers may have to wait some time for a lift on the road north out of Eldoret.

Cost   80/– per group. (Individual rates are probably negotiable, especially mid-week.)

Facilities Bar, restaurant and swimming pool. Campers can use the showers and toilets by the pool, although a bathroom in an unoccupied bungalow may be made available. Soy centre has dukas and hotelis.
Security Fence and askaris.
Bungalows 250/− double, bed and breakfast.
Bookings The Manager, Soy Country Club, PO Box 2, Soy. Tel: Soy 6.

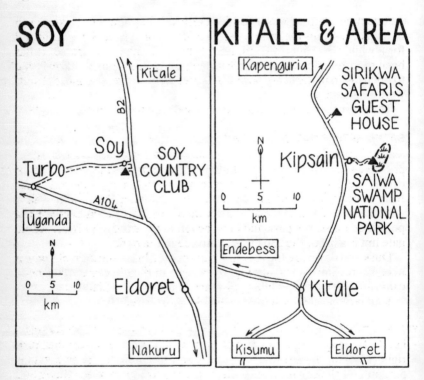

KITALE AND AREA

Kitale grew up around the station that marked the end of the railway line north from Nairobi, but since colonial days it has always been primarily a market town, the centre of one of Kenya's most fertile farming regions.

Kitale is the last big town before the main north road heads into the Cherangani foothills and the deserts of Turkanaland beyond. It is also a useful base for visits to Mount Elgon.

Nothing exists in the way of up-market accommodation, but a selection of B&Ls supply the basics, and the Sikh Temple takes guests. Kitale town has nowhere for camping either, but there are a number of sites in the area.

Access

Car   Kitale is on the main A1 Kisumu − The North road, about 70 km north of Eldoret. From Nairobi or Nakuru take the A104 north and then the B2 to Kitale. All of these roads are tarred.

Bus/Hitch   Kitale is regularly served by buses and matatus from all surrounding towns and by long distance buses from Nairobi, Kisumu and Lodwar. Passenger trains no longer run from Kitale.

At one time camping was possible at Grieve's Farm, about 10 km south of Kitale. It seems the farm was sold and renamed Blue Skies Farm and for a while was Kitale's youth hostel, but information is sparse. It has been reported, however, that a camping site called Grieve's Farm is due to open again in the same position. As we went to press no more details were available.

The two other campsites in the area are both to the north of Kitale.

SAIWA SWAMP NATIONAL PARK

Saiwa Swamp is the smallest national park in Kenya, gazetted to preserve the boggy habitat of the sitatunga, an aquatic antelope. These can be seen, along with De Brazza monkeys and many colourful birds, from wooden platforms among the trees overlooking the swamp. This is an ideal park for travellers without their own vehicle, as cars are not permitted inside the park and must be left at the warden's office. At the gate hut is a list of the 230 birds identified in the park.

Dusk and dawn are the best times to spot the birds and animals, which necessitates an overnight stop. Near the park office are two grassy campsites within easy walking distance of the viewing platforms.

Standard park entry fees are payable at the gate.

Position   From Kitale take the main A1 road north towards Kapenguria and Lodwar. After 20 km, before the small village of Kipsain, turn right (east) onto a dirt road (signposted). From here to the park gate is 5.5 km and the car park and offices are 0.5 km further on. Buses and matatus from Kitale to Kapenguria (or Lodwar) pass the junction, but from there you'll have to walk. Hitching out of Kitale might mean a long wait and a lift to the park would be unusual.

Cost   30/- ppn.

Facilities   Pit toilet. Water from the staff village. Firewood.

Security   No askaris, but no problems ever reported.

SIRIKWA SAFARIS GUEST HOUSE

Sirikwa Safaris Guest House is the home of a settler family, in a beautiful situation amongst farmland and pine trees. The guest house is an ideal place to stop over after exploring Mount Elgon or the northern deserts and also makes a possible base for visiting Saiwa Swamp or the Cherangani Hills.

Another of Sirikwa Safaris's attractions is the wide variety of birds that inhabit the area. Very knowledgeable, English-speaking, bird guides can be hired to accompany guests on short tours around the nearby forest and farmland, or around Saiwa Swamp National Park, or to go further afield to other birding areas such as Kisumu and Kakamega.

The guest house offers rooms and meals, and packed lunches can be provided. Fully furnished tents can be hired. Camping is on the large lawn behind the house.

Position   See directions to Saiwa Swamp above. Sirikwa Safaris Guest House is on the A1 road 6 km north of the Kipsain junction, 26 km north of Kitale. The guest house is signposted on the right (east) side of the road.
Cost   50/— ppn for camping.
Facilities   Drinking water, toilets, hot showers, fireplaces, firewood, kerosene lamps, mess tent in dry weather. Nearest dukas 2 km at Kesogon (South) or Merkwijit (North).
Security   Fence, night askari. Safe to leave tents during the day.
Rooms   600/— double, bed and breakfast.
Furnished tents   150/— ppn.
Bookings/Enquiries   For the guest house, book in advance through Lets Go Travel, Standard St, Nairobi.

THE CHERANGANI HILLS

The Cherangani Hills lie to the north-east of Kitale, between the main A1 Kitale — Lodwar road and the Kerio Valley, and is an excellent wild camping area both for backpackers and campers with cars. Do not be deceived by the name though; although the Cheranganis are not as rugged as some other Kenyan ranges, most of this 'hill'—country is above 2500 m, and the highest peak, Nagen, is 3581 m.

The Cheranganis receive good rains and the soil is fertile, so much of the lower hills are farmed and populated (by the Marakwet and Pokot peoples), but the high ground and the forested foothills offer a good number of camping places, especially in the north. In recent years the construction of the graded 'Cherangani Highway' (running from a junction just north of Kapenguria right through the hills down to Iten), and several smaller Rural Access Roads, has improved communication for the local people. This has also made access routes for backpackers simpler. A day or two's drive through the Cheranganis takes car-campers into some of the most spectacular hill-country in Kenya. Although some of the roads in the Cheranganis have been graded many are still very steep and 4WD is recommended.

For campers without a vehicle matatus run two or three times per week from Mukatano, near Kapenguria, to some of the lower settlements in the west, and connect Iten with some of the settlements in the south-east. A walk from one matatu terminus to another takes a couple of easy days walking, but may involve a wait of another day or two for a matatu.

Only one official campsite exists in the Cherangani region. In all other areas 'wild' camping is necessary. Water is available from streams except in the highest areas.

settlements it might be wise to ask permission, to let the local people know who you are. Alternatively, camp in secluded places.

For more information about hiking and camping in the Cherangani Hills see *Mountain Walking in Kenya*, *Backpacker's Africa – East and Southern*, or *Mountains of Kenya* (see page 45).

MARICH PASS FIELD STUDIES CENTRE

This provides residential and educational facilities for student groups, but is also open for independent travellers. The centre is situated next to a river and a wide variety of physical landscape, vegetation, wildlife and human lifestyles are within easy reach. This is an ideal base for walking and camping in the northern Cherangani Hills and the centre can provide guides for walkers or guards for campers who want to leave their vehicle in the hills. Bsic supplies and fresh foodstuffs are available from nearby *dukas*.

Position   From Kitale follow the main A1 road for approximately 100 km (tarred) through Mukatano (near Kapenguria) to the Marich Pass. Pass a junction on the right signposted Sigor and Tot. After a further 2 km turn right onto a dirt road to reach the field centre (signposted) after a further kilometre.

Cost   40/- ppn for camping.

Facilities   Clean water, toilets, showers, firewood, guards.

Bandas/Dormitories   70/- ppn.

Enquiries   Mr David Roden, PO Box 2454, Eldoret; Tel: (0321) 31541 or Nairobi 332067.

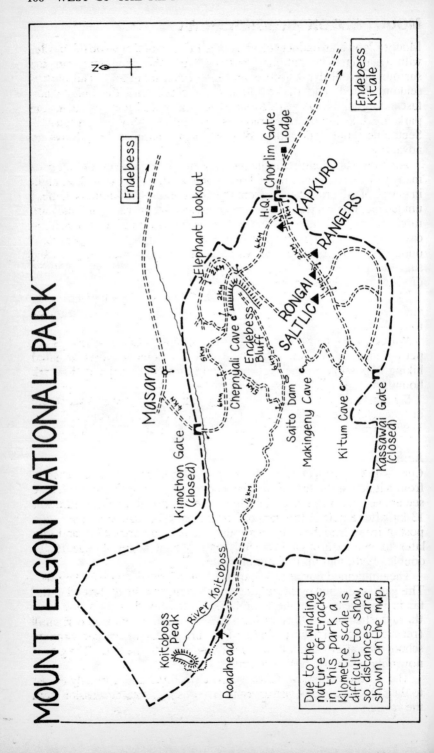

MOUNT ELGON NATIONAL PARK

MOUNT ELGON NATIONAL PARK

Mount Elgon is an extinct volcano in the far west of Kenya on the border with Uganda. The national park contains this mountain and the surrounding tall dense forests and high open moorland. The park is seldom visited, and this emptiness combined with the unique and fascinating landscape gives Mount Elgon a special feel. Roads in the park are bad in the rainy months of April — May and August — September, but cars with 4WD and high clearance are always an advantage.

An interesting feature of the park are the three large caves that over many years have been enlarged by elephants 'tusking' the walls at night in search of minerals missing from their diet. Sadly the numbers of these unique elephants have been severely reduced by poaching and they are rarely seen these days. However a daytime exploration of the large caves by torchlight reveals evidence of tusking and some pervasive odours; bat droppings if nothing else. (Recent scientific reports have suggested that the bat droppings may carry a disease similar to Weils disease carried in rats urine).

The distinctive cliffs of Endebess Bluff dominate much of the park, and Elephant Lookout offers excellent views over surrounding shambas towards the distant Cherangani Mountains.

Walking into the park is not allowed, although visitors with cars are permitted to leave their vehicles to visit the elephant caves. Isolated hiking is possible in the high moorland and peaks beyond the park boundary. (See *wild camping* section).

Signposts at junctions, caves and campsites are clear, except the distance shown to Koitoboss Peak is in fact only to the roadhead.

Standard national park entrance fees are payable at Chorlim Gate.

Access

Car   The only official way into the park is via Chorlim Gate, reached from Kitale via the tarred road to Endebess. (For directions to Kitale see above). Two routes to Chorlim Gate are possible: either turn left 13 km after Kitale at the signpost for the park; or turn sharp left at the post office in Endebess. Both are dirt roads in fair condition, and join later to climb through farmland, past Mount Elgon Lodge (900/- double, 1990) and up to Chorlim Gate.

The unmanned northern Kimothon Gate is for official vehicles only. This gate is reached by continuing on the unmade road at the end of the tar in Endebess, over the Koitoboss River, then left on a dirt road through shambas to Masara (also called Masaba) centre and sawmill (reached after 16.5 km). Follow this dirt road past Masara primary school then after 1 km follow a track on the left to the park. The gate is now only two poles beside the track.

The southern Kassawi Gate is also unmanned and normally closed to the public, although visitors can leave this way with permission from the rangers.

Bus/Hitch   For Chorlim Gate, matatus go as far as Endebess, then it is an 11 km walk to Chorlim Gate. Lifts are rare, but dukas supply sodas on route.

For Kimothon Gate (vehicle and pedestrian entry not permitted), matatus go from Kitale to Masara most days, weather and road conditions permitting. The matatus stop 4 km from the gate, and it's another 12.5 km to the nearest campsite at Kapkuro.

CAMPING

You need a car (or a lucky hitch) to get to any of the campsites in the park via Chorlim Gate, but with permission from the rangers you can camp for free outside the gate. Water and toilets are available and there is a small duka.

Cost   30/−ppn. Special campsites 300/−pw.

Kapkuro Public Campsite

This campsite has a beautiful setting in a grassy forest clearing where water buck and forest pigs visit at dusk, and the eerie call of colobus monkeys wake you in the morning.

Facilities   Water from a rain tank, pit toilet with thoughtful extras, firewood.

Rangers Public Campsite

Two small, secluded, seldom used forest glades.

Facilities   None.

Rongai Public Campsite

Another picturesque clearing visited by water buck, however you have to hunt for a flat place to pitch.

Facilities   Water from a stream at the bottom of the sloping field and plentiful firewood.

Saltlic Special Campsite

A grassy clearing deep in the forest, beside a bubbling stream. An idyllic place, however the 700 m of steep track down to the site is difficult in the wet. ('Saltlic' is not a misprint!)

Facilities   Stream water, firewood.

The Roadhead

At the end of the track up towards Koitoboss Peak there is room for three or four tents and vehicles. This site makes a good base for a one day excursion up to the crater, or a convenient starting point for longer backpacking expeditions. The site is unofficial and more information is supplied in the next section.

MOUNT ELGON WILD CAMPING

Mount Elgon offers excellent isolated moorland hiking in some of the most dramatic scenery in Kenya. At the centre of the mountain massif is a huge crater surrounded by a ring of peaks. On the crater floor, hot springs are evidence of the volcanic activity.

Although the highest peak on Mount Elgon at 14,000 feet (4321 metres) means that altitude sickness is unlikely, walking here is no less serious than on Mounts Kenya or Kilimanjaro. Hikers should have a reasonable amount of mountain experience and need to be completely self-contained, as there are no huts on the high moorlands and even water is not easy to find. A good tent and warm sleeping bag are recommended and a compass is essential as mists are common and paths sometimes indistinct. At least one companion is desirable as people, and therefore help, are sparse on the high moorlands and the lower forests.

Officially camping and walking is still not allowed in the area around the crater. Following the civil war in neighbouring Uganda rebel soldiers used to cross the crater on their way to steal from Kenyan villages on the lower slopes of Mount Elgon. Murder and other atrocities were frequent. No trouble of this sort has been reported since 1986, but the region cannot be pronounced totally safe, as armed poachers enter the park this way. Poaching is a big problem in this area and poachers are likely to be as dangerous as rebel soldiers. If you intend to reach the crater area you do so at your own risk, and with a certain amount of discretion.

Having said that, the days we spent hiking on Mount Elgon were some of the finest we have experienced anywhere in Africa. The walking was not strenuous, the scenery was beautiful and the air crystal clear. We seemed to have the entire crater to ourselves and in the three days we spent on the mountain we did not see a single person.

ACCESS ROUTES TO THE CRATER

1a The Park Route via Chorlim Gate (ie official), to the roadhead, and up to the Col south of Koitoboss Peak.
1b The Park Route via Kimothon Gate (unofficial), to the road-head.
2 The Masara Route, north of the park, and up to the Col.
3 The Kimilili Route, on the southern side of the mountain, to Lower Elgon Peak.

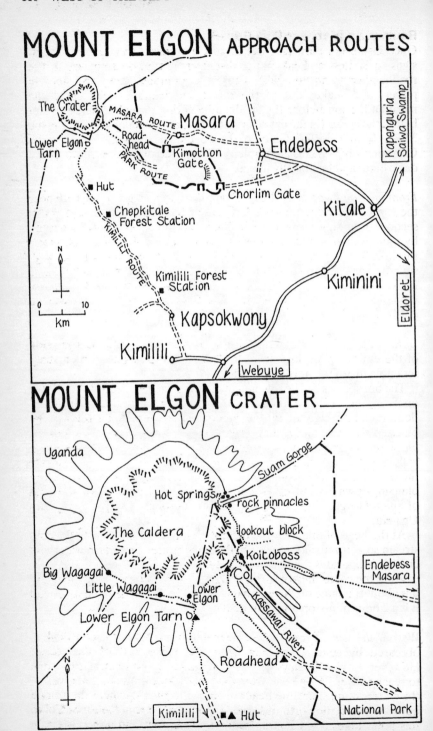

Routes 1a and 1b, The Park Routes

Once inside the park (see details in *Campsites Access* above) follow
signs to Koitoboss Peak (note: distances written on signs are to the
roadhead only, *not* to peak). The track is muddy, rocky and steep in
places, and snakes out of the forest and bamboo belts up to the
moorland. 1 km before the roadhead a spring provides the last water
before the crater (in the dry season this may not be reliable). Driving the
30 km from Chorlim Gate to the roadhead takes 1.5 – 3 hours.
Clearance and 4WD is advisable. Walking, the distance is more than a
day's hike, and technically illegal.

From the Roadhead to the Col   From the roadhead get to the path near
the top of the ridge on your left, either by scrambling up the rocky
section, or finding a way round it. The ridge path is obviously used more
by animals than humans but these are seldom seen. The path is clear and
the hike 2.5 – 3 hours to the col at the southern base of the large
squarish rocky buttress of Koitoboss Peak. On the col, flat places can be
found to pitch a tent. These are not particularly sheltered, but the sun
providing warmth at dusk and dawn is compensation. Frost and ice are
common at night.

Beyond the Col   Koitoboss Peak, the highest peak on the Kenyan side
of the crater, is an hour from the col. The top is gained by a steep
scramble up on the north-west side.

   The hot springs can be reached by skirting the base of Koitoboss Peak
on its western side, avoiding the tussock-jumping traverse of the crater
floor. Head through the rattling lobelia plants (*podos*) towards a rocky
block in the centre of a small gap in the crater wall (marked *lookout
block* on the crater map). From here you can look eastwards down
valleys to the hazy distant peaks of the Cheranganis. To the west, inside
the crater, the path becomes well-defined, crossing a flat section before
plunging down to wind left around impressive rock pinnacles to the head
of Suam Gorge. Cross the large stream via rocks to step illegally into
Uganda.

   At the head of Suam Gorge the hot spring water mixes with the cold
stream so you can choose your bath temperature. The warm water and
chill air invigorates the body sauna-style.

   From the col to the hot springs takes 2 – 2.5 hours walking time, and
it is about the same on the way back. From the col back to the roadhead
it is a 2 hour non-stop downhill march.

West of the Col   From the col near Koitobos, Lower Elgon Peak is
obscured by spurs projecting from the inside wall of the crater.
However, Lower Wagagai and 'Big' Wagagai can be seen. It is possible
to reach Lower Elgon peak from the Col by following the inner wall of
the crater round spurs and heads of valleys to the ridge near the domed
buttress just to the north of Lower Elgon Peak. From Koitobos Col to
this point takes 3 – 4 hours. Path very indistinct and non-existent in

On the col by Koitoboss peak, Mount Elgon.

places. From this point on the ridge you can reach the lake (Lower Elgon Tarn) via the Col between Lower Elgon Peak and Lower Wagagai. Allow 1 – 2 hours. From the tarn it's possible to descend via the Kimilili Route.

The Mount Elgon Map and Guide by A. Wielochowski is very useful. Available in Nairobi or from West Col Productions, UK.

Route 2, The Masara Route

From Masara centre (also called Masaba) continue up the dirt track. After 1 km ignore the left turn that leads to Kimothon Gate. Follow the track past the Forest Station until it turns into a very indistinct path. From here to the crater rim, south- west to the summmit of Koitoboss, is a long hike (25 km) and water supplies on the way are unreliable. Because walkers have not been permitted in this area until recently reports indicate that this route has been so little used that it is now overgrown and impassable.

If descending on the Park Route (after having come up the Kimilili Route) it is possible to go through the park and exit via Kimothon Gate, although this is technically illegal.

Route 3, The Kimilili Route

Kimilili is a small town to the south of Mount Elgon. It is best reached via the main Kitale – Webuye road (marked on some maps as the C43 but recently re-numbered the A1) and the C42 which runs between this main road and Kimilili. These roads are tarred and frequented by buses and matatus.

From Kimilili matatus climb then drop to Kapsakwony, the beginning of the route proper. It is best to leave Kimilili as early as possible in the morning to get on the route in good time. Therefore an overnight stop in Kimilili is recommended in one of a number of reasonable B&Ls in the town.

From Kapsakwony to the Hut Kaberua Forest Station (formerly Kimilili Forest Station) is 4.5 km north of Kapsakwony on a dirt road towards the mountain. Hikers are required to register at the forest ranger's office (fork right just before the wooden barrier) and pay a fee of 5/- per night.

Chepkitale Forest Station (now closed) lies 20 km further, on a dirt road which runs through dense forest, bamboo and open moorland. If you're driving, a 4WD vehicle is essential. It is possible to camp there, or sleep in one of the abandoned buildings. Firewood is plentiful, but water supplies uncertain: collect water on the way up from the stream crossed by a bridge about 3 km before Chepkitale.

About 7 km beyond the Forest Station is the 'Austrian Hut', rebuilt by Austrian and British volunteers in 1985 and sadly fallen again into disrepair, with its roof gone and most of the furniture burnt. However, the camping is excellent with water available from the stream 5 minutes walk down into the valley behind the hut. The track is not passable for vehicles much beyond this point.

From Kimilili Forest Station to the hut is a 3 hour drive or a long day's walk (about 10 hours). The rangers at Chepkitale Forest Station are friendly and would allow camping if you wanted to break the journey here.

From the Hut to the Lake   Continue up the track. The roadhead is reached after about 3 km or 1 hour. Just before the roadhead, a path branches off to the right (marked by a cairn). This path leads up the left side, then right side, then left again, of a ridge of rocky outcrops. The path then crosses the left shoulder, marked by a cairn, of a large squarish outcrop (Sudek). The path keeps to the left of Sudek, dropping steeply for a few metres, passing to the left of a gap containing a pinnacle with a hole at its base and the cliffs of Lower Elgon Peak. After crossing a section of bare rock it reaches the tarn which is hidden until the last minute when approached in this direction. Occasional cairns and white splashes of paint show the way. From the hut to the tarn is 3 – 4 hours.

There is some idyllic camping near the lake which makes an ideal base for excursions to other points on the southern side of the crater.

Beyond the Lake   From the lake it is possible to reach Lower Elgon Peak in about an hour. Follow cairns and a steep gulley to the top, which offers excellent views down into the crater and back towards Kakamega Forest, Eldoret and the Nandi escarpment.

It is also possible to reach Little Wagagai Peak on the crater rim to the north west of the lake, and ('Big') Wagagai Peak, the highest point on Mount Elgon and in Ugandan territory. Allow four hours to reach Wagagai from the Lake, and about the same for the return journey.

For fully equipped campers familiar with high altitude walking, another option is the spectacular circling of the crater rim, towards Koitoboss Peak on the north-east side of the crater, reached after 2 – 3 hours. From the col to the south of Koitoboss you can descend to the park roadhead and through the national park, or retrace the Masara Route described above down to Endebess.

Information on the Kimilili Route supplied by Dianne Bibby and Rienhold Scharf.

Maps and Guides
An official Uganda Survey Department map of Mount Elgon was printed in 1967. This might be available in the Survey Department on Harambee Avenue, Nairobi. It is useful for topography, although roads and other less permanent features are less reliably shown.

Useful guide-books include *Backpacker's Africa — East and Southern* and *The Mountains of Kenya*. More details in the *Guide Books* section.

On our trips from Kimilili up to the Elgon crater, the lake was always a favourite stopping point. Although it probably has other names we always used to call it the 'secret lake' because you never knew it was there until you were right on top of it. It's a still, beautiful place, with a movie-set appearance, sheltered from the cold winds that often blow on Mount Elgon.

We would advise walkers to leave Kimilili at sunrise to avoid rain and reach the hut before dark. Waterproofs are a must. Walking from the hut to the top should also be done very early in the morning so as to get a good view and return before any fog comes down. Only on one of three occasions did we come close to getting caught in the fog. But that was enough.

On this side of the mountain people might occasionally see a group of local guys running in a line as if on an army exercise. I was rather frightened when I saw them, suspecting that they were Ugandan cattle raiders. In fact they were local herdsmen who proved very helpful when we were lost. (Dianne Bibby and Rienhold Scharf, Kakamega, London and Germany)

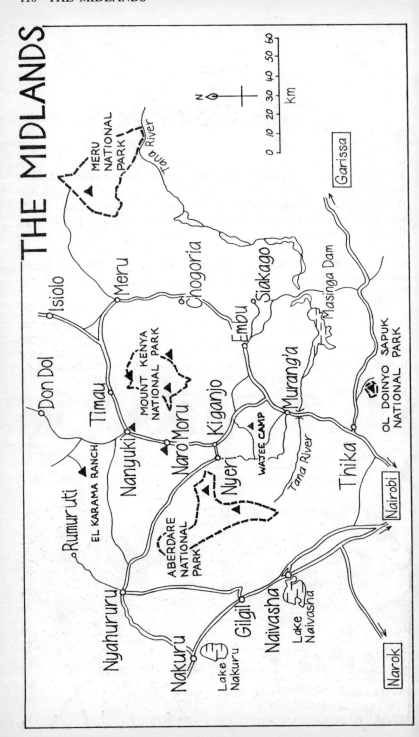

Chapter 11

The Midlands

The two main natural features of the Midlands are the massifs of Mount Kenya and the Aberdare Range. These mountains catch the clouds and the surrounding region enjoys reliable rainfall, full rivers and fertile soil. During colonial times this was seen as land ripe for settlement and the Europeans were given exclusive farming rights. Tea and coffee estates were established on the well watered slopes and the drier areas were used for wheat farming or cattle ranching. In the period before independence parts of the Midland region became known as the White Highlands.

The Midlands remain a farming area today, although much of the farmland has been divided up into smallholdings or *shambas*, but this varied region also has its share of attractions for the tourist. You can camp below the snow capped peaks of Mount Kenya, in the dense forests of the Aberdares, or in the dry bushland of Meru National Park. And whether you travel by car or bus most places are still within a day's journey of Nairobi.

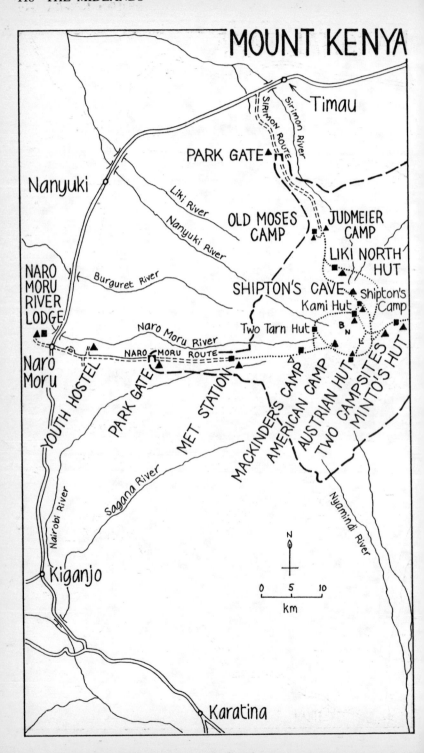

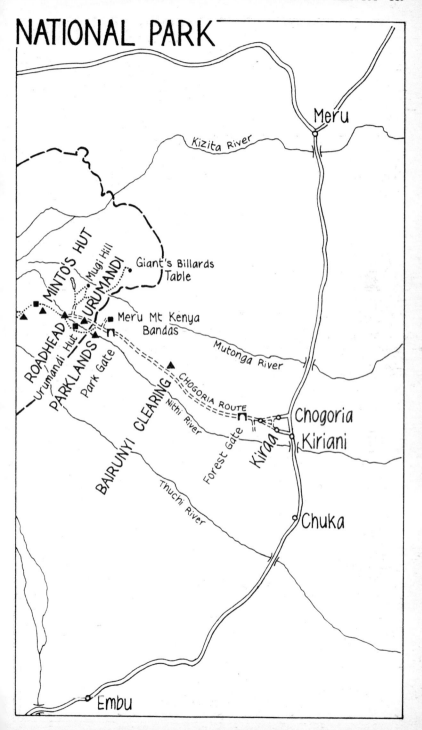

MOUNT KENYA NATIONAL PARK

The Mount Kenya National Park includes forest, open moorland, and many surrounding foothills as well as the rocky peaks of the mountain itself. Sited on the equator, but capped with snow and ice all year round, Mount Kenya is a wild and compelling place.

The twin summits of Bation and Nelion can only be reached by experienced technical climbers, but well trodden routes make Point Lenana, the walkers' peak, easily accessible. Unfortunately many people come ill-prepared for the sub-zero temperatures, or don't allow time to acclimatise, and so fail to reach the top or become too ill to appreciate the splendour of the dawn at 5,000 m.

Ascending Mount Kenya is a serious venture which claims lives every year. Even experienced mountaineers have lost their way in surprise mists or come to grief on the treacherous scree-slopes. But with suitable equipment, a steady ascent, and a good guide book you should have no problems.

Permanent camps and huts have been built along the main routes, but some are dilapidated, and others very crowded in the high season, so a tent on Mount Kenya has obvious advantages. The official campsites near the permanent camps and huts are all covered in this section. Many more possible camping places can be found along the routes, and some of the popular spots are also described here.

The best time to climb Mount Kenya is during the drier seasons of July – September and January – February, although the mountain can be attempted at any time of the year. During rainy months an early start means you can cover a good distance and pitch your tent before the regular afternoon downpour.

Standard National Park entrance fees apply. The park daily charge of 30/– ppn is paid at the gates, with additional overnight hut and camp fees payable at some sites.

Mountain expeditions organised by tour companies or hotels will use locally hired guides and porters. For independent campers, guides and porters are not obligatory or strictly necessary, although they can make the climb safer and easier for those unused to carrying loads at high altitude.

The popular routes on Mount Kenya have become very badly polluted in recent years. Thoughtless climbers have abandoned empty tins and other rubbish inside huts, or left toilet waste unburied at campsites, which is unsightly and can lead to water contamination and disease. Please carry off all rubbish, and encourage porters to do the same. Ensure that excrement and paper is buried deeply, well away from water sources. Real heroes will carry down rubbish that other slobs have left behind.

There are at least six routes up Mount Kenya and the three most common are covered here.

NARO MORU ROUTE

The Naro Moru route begins near the small town of the same name on the western side of Mount Kenya. The route is popular with independent hikers and tour companies as it's short, allows a quick ascent and has the easiest access by car and public transport.

The route is steep, especially after the Met Station. Don't be tempted to get a lift as high as possible and miss the relatively friendly gradient at first. Campsites are conveniently spaced and impressive views of the twin peaks are encouragement as you trudge nearer the top.

Porters and guides can be arranged at the Mount Kenya Guides and Porters Association Headquarters between Naro Moru town and the youth hostel, or where mentioned below.

Access
Car Naro Moru town lies on the A2 Muranga – Nanyuki road (tar) about 160 km north of Nairobi. From Naro Moru it's 16 km to the park gate along a dirt road. The park gate is signposted.
Bus/Hitch Buses run regularly between Nairobi or Nyeri and Nanyuki via Naro Moru. Hitching is possible on this road. A matatu runs from Naro Moru towards the youth hostel and occasional traffic all the way to the park gate makes hitching feasible, although you may have to pay.

Naro Moru River Lodge
A colonial-style country hotel, with rooms or self-catering cottages, built amongst tall trees and manicured gardens. The campsite and basic bunkhouses are set beyond the hotel in less leafy surroundings. The hotel organises several all-inclusive mountain safaris and can also arrange lifts to the park gate, or guides and porters for independent hikers.
Cost 40/- ppn.
Facilities Water and toilets. Bar and restaurant at the lodge.
Security Fence and askaris.
Bunkhouse 100/- ppn.
Bookings and enquiries PO Box 18, Naro Moru, Tel: Nairobi 337501/8, Nanyuki 22548.

Bantu Lodge/Mountain Rock Lodge
Recently renamed Mountain Rock Lodge, but better known as Bantu Lodge, it lies 8 km north of Naro Moru. Cottages and campsite. See page 140 for details.

Mount Kenya Youth Hostel
The original old farmhouse that served as a youth hostel burned down in 1988, but has been replaced by bandas and a campsite.
Cost Bandas 75/-ppn; camping 25/-; tent hire 30/-.
Facilities Showers, toilets, small cafeteria serving basic local food.
Security Askaris. Guides and porters can be arranged from here.
Bookings/Enquiries Nairobi Youth Hostel (see page 56).

Park Gate

The park gate is 8 km from the youth hostel. Camping is allowed here, if time is too short to reach the next camp at the Met Station.

Facilities   Water and toilets at the gate.

Met Station (3050 m)

The Met Station is at the end of the drivable track (difficult in wet conditions), 8 km from the park gate. The huts belong to the Naro Moru River Lodge and the campsite is on the grass nearby. Guides and porters can sometimes be hired here, but you'd be safer to arrange this lower down.

Cost   Camping is 30/− ppn, payable on arrival at the Met Station.

Facilities   Water, clean pit toilet.

Security   The only thieves to worry about are the monkeys.

Huts   125/− ppn. Own sleeping bag required.

Mackinder's Camp (4200 m)

Mackinder's Camp is about 6 hours uphill from the Met Station. The first half of this route slogs through the infamous vertical bog.

   The campsite is an area of hard flat soil near the Mackinder's Camp huts, now called Teleki Lodge, which also belong to the Naro Moru River Lodge.

   From Mackinder's to Austrian Hut and Top Hut takes 2 − 4 hours.

Cost   Camping is 15/− ppn.

Facilities   Stream water in pipe, toilet.

Hut   200/− ppn (students 150/− ppn).

American Camp

Flat area for camping a little to the north of the path 1 hour from Mackinder's Camp. Water from stream.

CHOGORIA ROUTE

The Chogoria Route begins near the small town of Chogoria on the eastern side of Mount Kenya. This is one of the longest routes up the mountain, but it is becoming increasingly popular as the Naro Moru Route gets over-used. The approach road to the park gate passes through thick forest, home to buffalo and elephant, but these are rarely encountered although the track is littered with odorous proof of their existence.

Visitors entering the national park via the Chogoria gate are required to pay concession fees (or 'track fees') as well as the standard national park entrance fees. This is for the up-keep of the track through the forest reserve which is the responsibility of the local council: Adult 10/−, Children 2/−, Vehicle 10/−, Camping 10/− ppn.

The national park boundary actually lies 3 km beyond the park gate. Thus it is not necessary to pay park entry fees if you are staying at the Meru Mount Kenya Bandas (self-catering cottages/lodge only 1 km beyond the gate) and returning directly without entering the national park.

Guides and porters can be arranged through the Chogoria Guest House in Chogoria town.

Recent reports are that the road from Chogoria to the park gate has deteriorated and in wet conditions it is difficult to get even a 4WD vehicle up there.

Access

Car   Chogoria town lies 2 km to the west of the B6 Embu – Meru road (tar) about 150 km north of Nairobi. From Chogoria town it's 6 km to the forest gate past scattered huts and shambas, and from the forest gate a further 23 km through the forest reserve to the park gate.

Bus/Hitch   Buses and matatus run regularly between Embu and Meru. Some go into Chogoria, but it may be necessary to get off at the Chogoria road junction (signposted) or the Kiraa road junction just north of Kiriani. Traffic up to the park gate is infrequent, so the chance of a lift is slight, however the walk is good for acclimatisation.

Chogoria, Kiriani or Kiraa have no campsites but do have some basic B&Ls and the slightly more upmarket Chogoria Guest House at Chogoria or the Transit Motel at Kiraa. In the past hikers have been allowed to camp at the Forest Gate Station: No facilities, no charge.

Bairunyi Clearing

Just over 14 km from the forest gate a large grassy clearing opens out on the right of the track. This clearing provides the only good camping space between the two gates as the forest is very dense and grows right up to the track. A stream runs in a valley below the site, a long walk through thick bush, so it's highly recommended you take your own water.

Park Gate/Parklands

Camping is not available at Meru Mount Kenya Bandas or at the park gate itself. The nearest site is a grassy clearing 0.5 km beyond the gate, sometimes called Parklands.

Turn sharp left after the gate (ie not to the Bandas), then fork left again onto an unclear track up a small hill and round to the left.

Facilities   Toilet, hut shelter. Water may not be reliable but can be obtained from the gate or the Bandas.

Urumandi Hut and Campsite

Take the track to Parklands Campsite and continue on for about 3 km. The hut belongs to the Mountain Club of Kenya and camping is possible nearby. A path rejoins the main route above the roadhead.

Urumandi Special Campsite

A spacious site beneath trees in the beautiful Urumandi Glade.

Take the track towards the roadhead. The special campsite is signposted left 100 m off the main track, 2.4 km from the park gate.

Facilities   Water, pit toilet, hut shelter.

Roadhead Campsite (3300 m)

The roadhead is 7 km from the park gate at the end of a steep rough track. There is a limited amount of open space here for camping. Water from nearby stream or falls. No other facilities.

Day hikes from the Roadhead Campsite to Mugi Hill and the Giant's Billiards Table provide good acclimatisation if time allows.

Minto's Hut (4290 m)

Minto's is 6 hours walk from the roadhead, with no water available en route. The old hut was dismantled when the new hut was completed in 1988. It has been suggested that the new hut is little better than the old one; it is dirty, draughty, and the roof leaks. Camping is possible amongst the nearby stepped tarns, which provide water.

Austrian Hut is 2 − 3 hours walking from Minto's. The hour's scramble up icy scree from here to Point Lenana is less hazardous early in the morning.

Other campsites

Between 1.5 and 2 km from Minto's Hut various flat grassy places on the right and left of the path give possible campsites. Streams provide water, but slow run-off means the ground is very wet after rain.

We approached Mount Kenya via the Chogoria Route. It was a long walk from the town right up to the park gate in one day, but if we'd broken the walk at Bairunyi Clearing we would have needed to carry more water. A friendly ranger at the park gate invited us to camp on the grassy path between the rangers' huts and the gate itself, which was fine. Mintos Hut cannot be recommended − it is cold and leaks like a sieve. While we were there two Japanese climbers put their tent up inside the hut to keep warm and dry! (John Simmons, Britain)

Beware the wind on Mount Kenya! I've got one of those fancy new free-standing geodesic tents, which are usually ideal for camping on loose surfaces. I was with a group camping near Minto's and I'd taken all my gear out of the tent and had just finished unpegging when a huge gust of wind got underneath and carried it off UP the mountain, rolling and bouncing along like a huge balloon. We were already suffering from the altitude and had to send some of the porters off to catch it. They thought it was a great joke, running uphill in pursuit of a runaway tent, but managed to bring it back luckily still in one piece and undamaged. (Mike Wood, Nairobi and Scotland)

SIRIMON ROUTE

The Sirimon Route begins near the small town of Timau where the main road crosses the River Sirimon on the northern side of Mount Kenya. The least used of the three main routes, it is perhaps the most strenuous due to a more hilly approach.

The route approaches the summits from the north, so walkers need to pass to the east of the main peaks and climb Point Lenana from Austrian Hut. The direct route to Lenana from Kami Hut involves some very steep scrambling and can be very hazardous; for experienced mountain walkers only.

Access

Car Timau town lies on the main A2 Nanyuki – Isiolo road (tar). The dirt road up to the park gate leaves the main road south-west of Timau, 1 km from the large new road bridge over the Sirimon River, 16 km from Nanyuki, 65 km from Meru. The park gate is 9 km from the main road (signposted).

The dirt road from the junction to the park gate is steep and rocky in places but passable for all vehicles. With 4WD it's possible to drive about 10 km beyond the gate to the roadhead.

Bus/Hitch Buses and matatus run regularly along the A2 between Nanyuki and Meru or Isiolo. It will be easier for a matatu to drop you at the junction. Hitching is no problem on the main road, but you'll probably have to walk up to the park gate.

Park Gate Campsite

The campsite is near the gate buildings in a grassy clearing.
Facilities Water from gate, pit toilet.

Roadhead Campsite (3350 m)

The roadhead for 2WD vehicles is 8 km (2 – 3 hours walking, 1 hour driving) from the park gate, where a stream crosses the track. A further 2 km (1 hour walking, 20 minutes driving) is the 4WD roadhead. Judmeier Camp (owned by Bantu Lodge) is sited here and allows tents to be pitched on a rather exposed campsite nearby. This costs 30/– ppn.

Liki North Hut (3990 m)

This hut is near the top of the Liki Valley before the steep ascent to the peaks, about 4 hours walking from the 4WD roadhead campsite. Camping is possible by the stream in the valley beyond the hut.

Shipton's Cave Campsite (4100 m)

This site (7 hours from the 4WD roadhead, 3.5 hours from Liki North Hut) is at the head of Mackinder's Valley, on the last good bit of flat ground before the top. The campsite is below the rocky outcrops of Shipton's Cave, a bad bivvy in an emergency.

Further up the valley is Shipton's Camp, a tented camp run by Bantu Lodge. Camping is permitted here, although unusual, and costs 30/– ppn.

From Shipton's Cave to Austrian Hut takes 4.5 hours.

Kami Hut (4430 m)

For backpackers doing the circuit route of the peaks camping is possible at Kami Hut, which is 2 hours from Shipton's Cave. The hut is very basic and used mostly by porters.

MAPS AND GUIDES

The official Survey of Kenya maps of Mount Kenya are unobtainable in Nairobi. The only up-to-date map available is *Mount Kenya 1 : 50,000 Map and Guide*, by Andrew Wielochowski and Mark Savage. (Full details in *Maps* section.)

Recommended guides books are:
East Africa International Mountain Guide, Andrew Wielochowski,
Guide To Mount Kenya and Mount Kilimanjaro, Iain Allen,
Backpacker's Africa — East and Southern, Hilary Bradt.
(Full details in *Books* section.)

ABERDARE NATIONAL PARK.

The Aberdare National Park contains a wide variety of landscapes ranging from dense indigenous forest to high moorland and mountain peaks. Animals are plentiful, particularly in the Salient area which includes a rhino sanctuary and the famous lodges Treetops and The Ark. Rainfall is high on the Aberdare range, and the park is closed in the heaviest rains. The driest months are August − September and December − February but it can get very cold all year round. The Aberdare range has officially been renamed Nyandarua, but as yet this name is not widely used.

There are a great many tracks around the park, especially in the Salient. Directions can usually be found painted on white rocks at junctions.

Standard national park entry fees are payable at all gates.

Access

Car   The main routes into the park are via Nyeri, about 160 km north of Nairobi on the main B5 towards Nyahururu. These roads are tarred all the way.

There are six public gates into the park, and two private ones serving Treetops and The Ark. You cannot reach these lodges in your own vehicle.

From Nyeri, the Salient can be approached via Ruhuruini Gate or Wandaris Gate, and the Chania Falls area via Kiandongoro Gate.

The park can be approached from the Nyeri − Nyahururu road in the north via Shamata Gate or Rhino Gate, or from Naivasha or Gilgil in the west via Mutubio Gate. The steepest section of this route, formerly impassable in the rains, is now tarred.

Vehicles with 4WD are advisable as all roads in the park are unmade. To enter the Salient area collect a key from your gate of entry and return it as you leave.

Bus/Hitch   Nyeri is served by numerous buses from Nairobi, but no public transport runs to any of the gates. Hitching into the park is very difficult.

Walking   To walk in the park you must be part of a group and pre-arrange the trip with the warden. You will be assigned a guard.

CAMPING

Camping in the Aberdare National Park has been severely restricted since some campers were attacked by aggressive lions in the early 1980s. Rumours abound concerning these man-eaters, but it seems that the release of some semi-tame lions used in a film were the cause of the problem. It is uncertain whether the campers were attacked by these beasts, hungry and unafraid of humans, or by the other lions reacting against encroachments on their territory, but the attacks resulted in the closure of most campsites outside the Salient and limitations for walkers on the high moorlands.

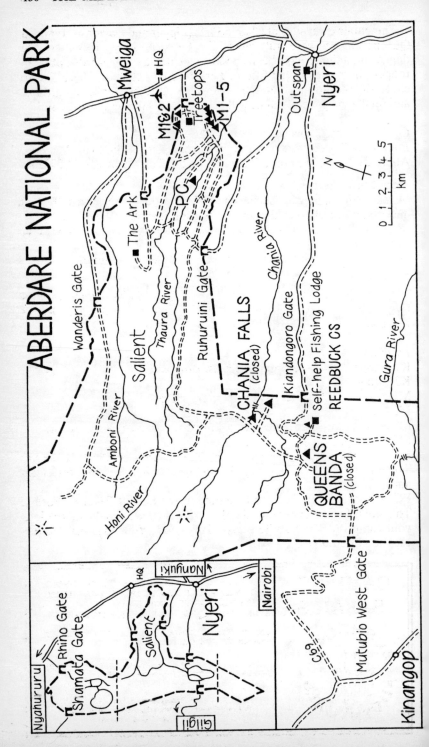

The public campsites at Chania Falls (Upper and Lower sites) and at Queens Banda were still closed in January, 1990. However, the dangerous animals have been shot or relocated and the warden plans to reopen these sites in the future. Park rangers will camp there first to check the conditions, then the sites will be used by competent groups, and finally the general public will be admitted if the tests prove safe!

Cost   30/− ppn. Special campsites 300/− psw.
Booking   To book walking and special campsites write to the Warden, Aberdare National Park, PO Box 22, Nyeri, Tel: Nyeri (0171) 59024.

Reedbuck Campsites
A new site, near the Self Help Fishing Lodge, and the only high moorland site open at the time of writing (January 1990).
Facilities   Firewood, toilets and water (no showers). Wet weather shelter. Take all food.
Security   Two banda workers are based here permanently.

Special Campsites
The Salient area contains eight special campsites which vary in remoteness and facilities; two at Kiguri (shortened to K1, K2), five at Muringato (M1 − M5), and Prince Charles (PC).

Facilities
K1 − toilet, borehole water (officially drinkable).
K2 − toilet.
M1 − toilet, river water tank (boil for drinking).
M2 − as M1.
M3 − none, but near enough to M1 and M2 to collect water by car.
M4 − as M3.
M5 − none. Perhaps the wildest of these seven sites, it overlooks the Treetops borehole with its nightly baited visits from buffalo, forest pig and elephant.
PC − none. A very secluded clearing in the Salient Riverine Forest. This site is for the experienced only, as inquisitive animals wander into your campsite. The birdlife is especially good. Your first visit there is escorted by a ranger.

WAJEE CAMP

This is a newly established campsite, in the eastern foothills of the Aberdares, well away from the usual tourist destinations. Despite the relatively dense rural population the area is also renowned for its birds. In the nearby forest live vervet monkeys and porcupines. A nature trail is being developed and visits to a nearby coffee plantation and factory can also be arranged.

Access

Car   Wajee Camp is outside the small centre of Mihuiti. The nearest large town is Karatina, on the main A2 Nairobi – Nanyuki road, 125 km north of Nairobi. The best approach is via Thika and Sagana, avoiding Maranga. From Karatina follow the main road north for 2 km towards Nyeri. Take the first tarred road on the left, towards Othaya, and follow it for about 14 km to rach Makurweini, then turn left on a dirt road to reach Mihuiti after a further 3 km.

Bus/Hitch   Buses and matatus run regularly between Nairobi and Nyeri via Karatina. Hitching on this road is possible. Local matatus run between Daratina and Makurweini, occasionally going on to Mihuiti.

Position   To reach Wajee Camp pass through Mihuiti centre and continue on the dirt road for 0.5 km. At a fork take the right turn and Wajee Camp is the next gate on the left.

Cost   30/- ppn

Facilities   Water, pit toilet.

Security   Askari

Bookings/Enquiries   Great Expeditions Ltd, Nairobi (see page 15).

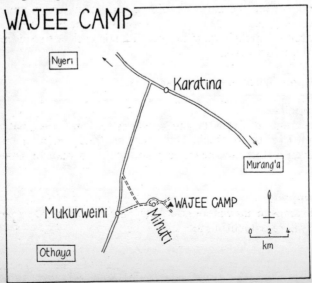

OL DOINYO SAPUK NATIONAL PARK

Ol Doinyo Sapuk is a small national park about 50 km to the north-east of Nairobi. Its size and accessibility makes the park popular with day-trippers, especially at weekends.

The park contains Ol Doinyo Sapuk mountain, also called Kilima Mbogo, (meaning 'mountain shaped like a cow'), and little else. Game is scarce, but views from the track winding up towards to the summit are excellent.

A series of violent robberies over the last few years means an armed guard accompanies each vehicle entering the park.

Standard national park entrance fees are payable at the gate.

Access
Car   Ol Doinyo Sapuk is about 25 km east of the industrial centre of Thika. The only route into the park is via the village of Kilima Mbogo 4 km south of the main A3 Thika − Garissa road. The park gate is signposted. The road is tarred as far as the Kilima Mboga junction, and drivable dirt track 7 km to the park gate. Inside the park a powerful 4WD car is needed to reach the top, as the track is steep and badly maintained in places.
Bus/Hitch   Buses and matatus run from Thika along the road towards Garissa; ask to get off at the Kilima Mboga junction. An irregular local service runs from the junction to Kilima Mboga centre, and from there it's a 3 km walk to the park gate. Hitching out of Thika is OK, but most vehicles going into the park are likely to be full. Walking is not permitted inside the park.

CAMPING
Camping high on the mountain is not allowed. There are two public campsites inside the park near the gate, and a special campsite outside the park 200 m from the gate. Usually special campsites in national parks are remote and secluded. This confused situation is probably due to people rarely camping here, either because it is so close to Nairobi or because of the security risk.

Cost   30/− ppn. Special campsite 300/− psw.

Public Campsites
Camping is permitted next to the gate buildings, and on a grassy patch of ground about 1 km up the track. There is a tap at the gate but no other facilities. Even at the sites near the gate security cannot be guaranteed.

Special Campsite
The special campsite has water and toilets, and also doubles as a picnic site. Security here is doubtful, too.

Between the main road and Kilima Mbogo centre are **Fourteen Falls**, a group of waterfalls on the heavily polluted River Athi. These are impressive in the wet season, and perversely interesting when the river is low and large clouds of detergent float high above the water.

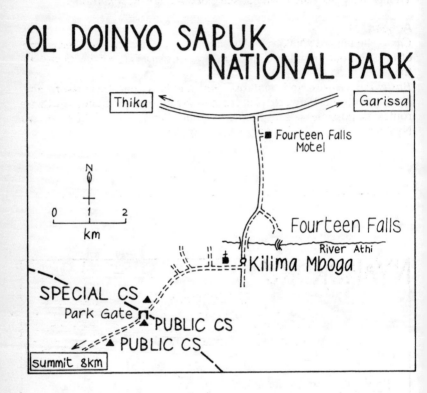

Hitching turned out to be the way to go, beyond all doubt. Not only did we easily get rides, but we got taken into homes, served food, bought beer, and often people would go out of their way to drop us off where we needed to be. We went all the way from Nairobi to Lake Turkana and back to Nakuru in private vehicles. We only paid for one ride (50/− each Lodwar to Kitale in a lorry). We even slept in the back of a lorry one night − quite an experience! (Florence Williams, USA)

NYAHURURU

Nyahururu is at the northern end of the Aberdare highlands, just a few kilometres north of the equator. The explorer Joseph Thomson discovered and named the impressive 75 m waterfall in 1883, and the colonial farming centre that became established there was called Thomson's Falls. The town has since been renamed Nyahururu.

Access

Car   The main B5 Nakuru – Nyeri road goes round the northern flank of the Aberdare highlands through Nyahururu. This road is tarred all the way.

Bus/Hitch   Buses and matatus run regularly between Nyeri and Nyahururu, and between Nakuru and Nyahururu. Hitching on these routes is possible with patience. Public transport and lifts on the Nyahururu – Nanyuki road are less frequent.

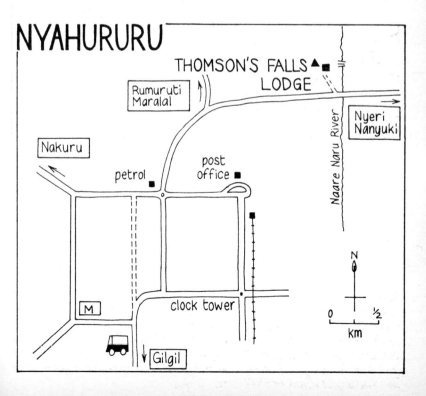

THOMSONS FALLS LODGE

Thomsons Falls Lodge has a rural atmosphere with panelled walls and polished floorboards, and a roaring fire in the bar. It is surrounded by pleasant gardens, but views of the falls are spoilt by a row of souvenir stalls.

The campsite is in a grassy garden behind the lodge.

Position   The lodge is on the north-east side of town, on the north of the Nyeri road, about 1 km from the centre.
Cost   40/- ppn.
Facilities   Toilets, water, firewood. Hot showers in the Lodge.
Security   Fence, askari, lights.

LAIKIPIA CLUB, Rumuruti

Rumuruti is on the C77 road from Nyahururu to Maralal and the east side of Lake Turkana, about 40 km north-east of Nyahururu. The road is tarred as far as Rumuruti then graded to Maralal.

In the past some travellers have camped at the old colonial-style Laikipia club in Rumuruti, but whether this is a regular arrangement is unknown. Facilities seem to be variable, and prices negotiable.

NANYUKI AREA

Located on the north-western edge of the Mount Kenya massif, Nanyuki was a trading centre and market town during the settler days and still retains a somewhat colonial atmosphere today. It is also a base for the Kenyan Air Force, and a training centre for the British Army.

Nanyuki has a market and plenty of shops, plus a selection of cheap B&Ls, a couple of slightly more up-market hotels, and a cheap but dilapidated youth hostel at the Emanuel Parish Centre.

To the south and east of Nanyuki the land rises towards the fertile foothills of Mount Kenya, while dropping away to the Laikipia Plains in the west and the semi-desert Samburulands to the north.

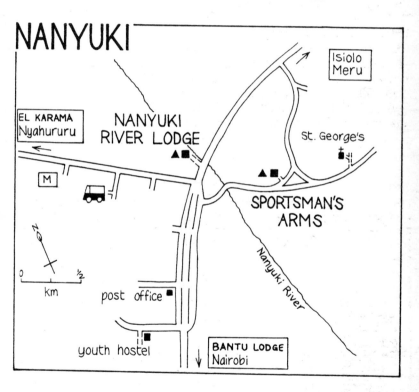

Access

Car The main A2 Nairobi – Isiolo – Moyale road passes through Nanyuki, 190 km north of Nairobi. This road is tarred as far as Isiolo.
Bus/Hitch Buses and matatus run regularly along the main road between Nairobi and Isiolo or Meru, via Nanyuki. Traffic is frequent and hitching is no problem.

There are two campsites in Nanyuki town itself, plus El Karama Ranch 40 km to the north-west, and Bantu Lodge 16 km to the south.

NANYUKI RIVER LODGE

The Nanyuki River Lodge is a group of self-contained cottages with a swimming pool, bar and restaurant. The campsite is a small secluded grassy area near the swimming pool.

The lodge organises walking trips on Mount Kenya, mainly on the Sirimon Route, and can advise on routes, guides and porters for independent hikers.

Position   Nanyuki River Lodge is on the north side of town, clearly signposted on the left of the road towards Isiolo.
Cost   30/– ppn.
Facilities   Water, toilets, showers, swimming pool. Bar and restaurant at the lodge.
Security   Fence and askari.
Cottages   500/– double, self-catering.
Bookings and Enquiries   PO Box 101, Nanyuki, Tel: 22736.

THE SPORTSMAN'S ARMS

The Sportsman's Arms was a country club in colonial days, but its collection of wooden cottages are somewhat rundown now, although the bar and restaurant hang on to an air of faded elegance. Camping is allowed on the lawns between the cottages, but there are no facilities specifically for campers.
Position   The Sportsman's Arms is on the east side of town on a small road heading towards some farms and the church.
Cost   50/– ppn, but this may be negotiable.
Facilities   No fires allowed. Campers are given a bathroom in a cottage to use.
Security   Fence and askari.
Cottage   400/– double, bed and breakfast.

EL KARAMA RANCH

El Karama is a private ranch combining domestic and wild animals. Visitors are encouraged to walk rather than drive around the ranch, and bird walks can be arranged. The early morning views of Mount Kenya across the plains are an unexpected bonus. El Karama is difficult to reach without your own transport as the house and campsite are at the centre of the ranch 10 km from the nearest road and public transport.

The campsite and bandas are in a picturesque setting among acacia trees by a river where swimming is possible, despite the worrying presence of shy hippos.

EL KARAMA RANCH

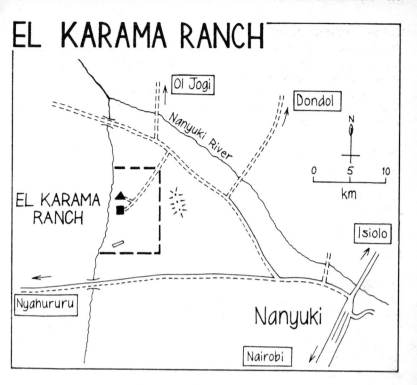

Position   El Karama is a 42 km drive from Nanyuki. Leave Nanyuki on the Nyahururu road, then fork right after 9 km towards Naibor. Follow the Naibor road for another 23 km. El Karama is not signposted, but look for three sign boards saying 'Ol Jogi – No Shooting' and turn left here. It's then another 10 km through ranch land to the house and campsite.

Report to the house before going to the campsite.

Cost   25/– ppn.

Facilities   Water, pit toilets, bucket showers (hot water can be arranged). Kerosene lamps can be hired. Take all your own food.

Security   Askaris on guard 24 hours, although there is very little risk of theft in this area.

Bandas   New, well kept and a bargain at 35/– ppn. Beds and other equipment can be hired.

Bookings and enquiries   Mr I.G.P. Grant, El Karama Ranch, PO Box 172, Nanyuki, Tel: Laikipia 34Y2. More information available at Let's Go Travel, Standard Street, Nairobi, where bookings can also be made.

BANTU LODGE/MOUNTAIN ROCK LODGE

Based on the country club design, with cottages built around a central bar and restaurant area. Being recently constructed it lacks the old colonial atmosphere found in similar establishments. Popular with locals and with safari companies, evenings in the bar can be lively if a group is passing through.

The lodge organises treks on Mount Kenya, and also offers guided day walks and horse rides in the area.

The campsite is on a large grassy lawn.

Position   Bantu Lodge is on the east side of the main A2 road, 8 km north of Naro Moru, 16 km south of Nanyuki, near the small village of Utamanduni. Look for a painted gateway, a mural of Mount Kenya on the fence and two huge carved wooden figures. From the main road to the Lodge is about a kilometre along a private road.

Cost   40/– ppn.

Facilities   Toilets, hot showers, hot bath (with limited privacy!), kitchen. Bar and restaurant in the lodge.

Security   Fence, askari, lights.

Cottage   300/– double, self-catering.

Bookings and enquiries   PO Box 333, Nanyuki; Tel: Naro Moru (01772) 2098/9. Also at Aardvark Safaris Ltd, IPS Building, Kimathi St, Nairobi (next to the New Stanley Hotel), or at Special Camping Safaris (see below).

MERU NATIONAL PARK

Meru National Park is off the itinerary of most safari companies, and is seldom reached by independent tourists, but here visitors can experience true wilderness seldom found in the other more popular parks. Elsa the lion of *Born Free* was raised here by George and Joy Adamson.

The low-level tourism, and maybe the high-level poaching that plagues this park, means animals are shy and tend to vanish before you've focused the zoom lens. Reticulated giraffe can be seen though, and Meru is the only East African home of the white rhino, even though the giant beasts are confined to corrals and a 24−hour guard.

Campsites have been designated throughout the western area of the park, giving intrepid campers many opportunities to invade a good cross section of habitats.

Standard national park entrance fees are payable at all gates.

Access
Car The main route into the park is along the C91 from Meru via Murera Gate. The tar extends to within 30 km of the park. From there the road is steep but drivable in the dry season. Inside the park, a maze of tracks makes most of the western area easily accessible, although drifts (fords) make some roads difficult in the wet. Cars are frequently swept off the slippery surfaces in the rainy season especially at Rhino, Fig Tree and Rattia Drifts.

It is also possible to enter via Ura Gate after a long hard drive along the C92 Meru − Tunya road (dirt) and another minor track via Gatunga. This route is indistinct and seldom used.

Bus/Hitch Buses and matatus run regularly to Meru from Nairobi or Embu, and from Nanyuki. From here there are occasional matatus running towards Maua town and Murera Gate, but hitchers will have to rely on tourist traffic as walking inside the park is not allowed.

CAMPING
Cost 30/− ppn. Special campsites 300/− psw.

Murera Gate Public Campsite
Position Near the gate buildings.
Facilities Water, toilet.

Park Headquarters Public Campsite
Position The park HQ is in the centre of the park. The campsite is in a pleasant setting beside a wooded stream.
Facilities Toilet, shower.
The white rhino corral is nearby.

MERU NATIONAL PARK
WESTERN AREA

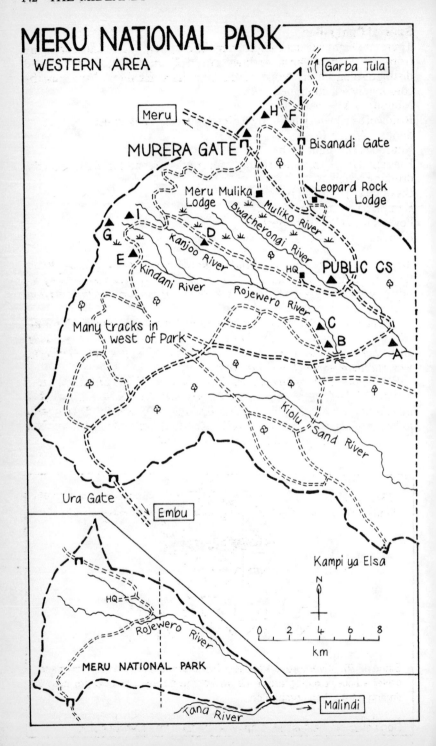

Garba Tula

Meru

MURERA GATE

H F

Bisanadi Gate

Meru Mulika Lodge

Leopard Rock Lodge

Muliko River

Bwatherongi River

I

G

D

Kanjoo River

E

Kindani River

HQ

Rojewero River

PUBLIC CS

C

Many tracks in west of Park

B

A

Kiolu Sand River

Ura Gate

Embu

Kampi ya Elsa

N

0 2 4 6 8
km

HQ

Rojewero River

MERU NATIONAL PARK

Tana River

Malindi

Special Campsites

There are eight special campsites in different types of location ranging from dry lowland bush to high forest. Each site has a name and distinguishing letter. None of the sites have facilities. You must be completely self contained.

Mugunga (A) − very dry.

Rojewero (B) − dry bush, by Rojewero River, seldom used.

Simba (C) − as B.

Kanjoo (D) − light bush.

Kindani (E) − remote setting, forested, stream for bathing, take drinking water.

Bisanadi (F) − light bush.

Kampi Ya Nyati (G) − as E.

Fever Tree (H) − light bush.

Kithanga (I) − as E.

Meru is by far the most beautiful of all the parks we camped in. When we were there we were the only tourists in the park. Unlike many of the other parks, a three day stay is the minimum amount of time anyone should plan to stay there.

Because the park is huge, we suggest that a guide be hired. The Tana River Circuit requires two rangers (by order of the assistant warden), and other circuits only require one. The price is 30/- per run. A 100/- tip was standard throughout our tour.

We would like to recommend the ranger Noor Sheik. he is a wonderful guide and truly loves his park and the animals. Also when travelling around the park, keep an eye out for poachers. They appear to be present in large numbers and the rangers would like to know where they are spotted.   (Linda Brown, NY, USA)

THE NORTH

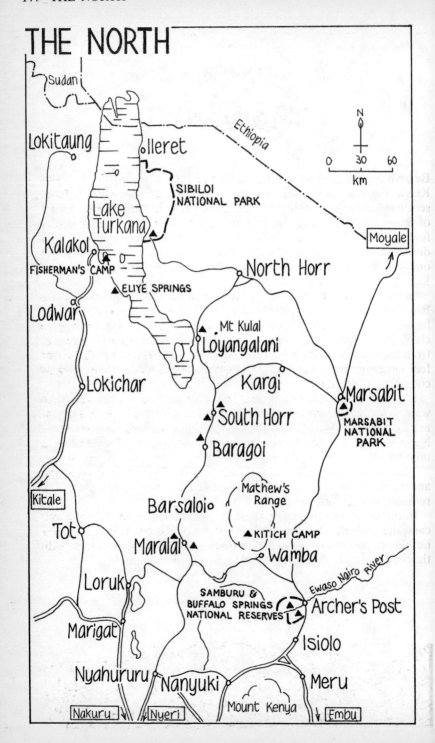

Chapter 12

The North

Beyond the forested mountains and fertile hills of western and central
Kenya the land drops surprisingly steeply to hot sparsely inhabited
scrubland, and beyond this the land gives way to the vast empty deserts
of the north. This is a region way off most visitors' itineraries and very
few southern Kenyans ever venture this far, unless to do business in a
distant market or else guard some isolated frontier police post. And yet
one look at a map will show that the north covers more than half of
Kenya's total land area.

In the north-west of this region Lake Turkana, the largest of Kenya's
Rift Valley lakes, is a thin ribbon of blue cutting through the parched
landscape. In the centre Mount Marsabit, high enough to form its own
clouds, is another oasis in the desert. But to the east there is no relief
from the endless sands except the few desert towns whose inhabitants
feel closer to their kinsmen in neighbouring Somalia than to their
compatriots 'down in Kenya'.

Lake Turkana attracts a growing number of visitors each year who
want to see something of the other side of Kenya. Particularly popular
are overland camping safaris organised by various companies in
Nairobi. To cater for these, campsites have been established at a
number of points along the common routes.

The northern national reserves at Samburu, Buffalo Springs, Shaba
and Marsabit all have campsites, and even Sibiloi National Park, the
remotest of them all, has a place to pitch your tent.

In the north-eastern region there is nothing in the way of organised
campsites, which takes it outside the scope of this book. In fact there's
nothing in the way of organised tourism at all, although for those with
the time and inclination this would be its very attraction.

LAKE TURKANA, THE WESTERN SHORE

Lodwar, the largest town on the west side of Lake Turkana, used to be a staging post for overland travellers going between Kenya and Sudan, diverting from the once popular 'Nile Route'. The value of this route, avoiding Uganda, was realised by the Kenyan government and a tarred road now winds through the Cherangani Hills and runs straight across the desert joining Lodwar with the rest of the country to the south.

The civil war in southern Sudan put an end to traffic crossing this border and at present very few tourists and travellers come this way.

For those who do, Lodwar has a few basic B&Ls, a market, some dukas and two campsites within striking distance of the town.

Access

Car   Lodwar is just under 300 km north of Kitale. The only viable route for vehicles is on the main A1 Kitale – Lodwar, now tarred all the way. On the desert plains beyond the Cherangani Hills this road crosses numerous dry river beds which may become suddenly impassable during the rainy season (April/May).

Bus/Hitch   At least one bus each day runs between Kitale and Lodwar. Hitchers with the usual supply of patience should be able to get a lift, although truck drivers on this route will expect payment.

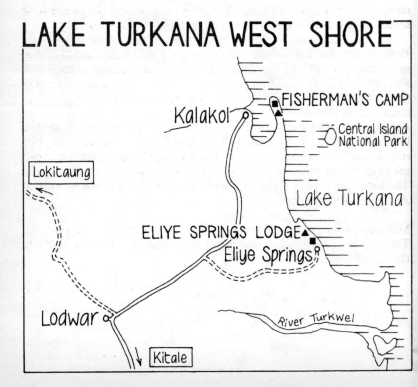

ELIYE SPRINGS LODGE, Eliye Springs
Eliye Springs Lodge used to be a popular sport-fishing centre but has now fallen on hard times. Wood and palm leaf bandas can be rented or just pitch your tent in the sand nearby. The lodge has a bar but no electricity, and a duka in the nearby village sells basic supplies. Fresh fish is usually available. Due probably to its lack of visitors the lodge has a very relaxed atmosphere which some people find appealing.

Position   Eliye Springs is about 40 km directly due east of Lodwar, although it's further by road. Take the new tarred road north towards Lokwa Kangole for about 30 km, then turn right (south-east) on to a dirt track. Follow this track for about 35 km down to the lake and Eliye Springs village. The lodge is on the north side of the village. Hitching may be possible; a number of aid organisations operate in this area, and a matatu makes the journey about four times per week.
Cost   20/− ppn, although negotiable for groups and long stays.
Facilities   Water, toilets. Showers are unreliable, far better is the warm spring waterfall between the lodge and the village.
Security   None, although problems seem unlikely.

FISHERMAN'S CAMP, Ferguson's Gulf
Fisherman's Camp, also called the Lake Turkana Angling Lodge, is a fairly up-market hotel catering mainly for week-end guests who fly in direct from Nairobi. Although the lodge has no official campsite it seems no objection is made if campers pitch on the beach nearby.

Position   Ferguson's Gulf is on the western lake shore about 70 km north-east of Lodwar. The new tarred road runs from Lodwar to Lokwa Kangole and Kalakol. From Kalakol it's a 5 km walk around the bay (not as far as it seems on the map since the lake waters have dropped considerably) to the lodge.
Facilities   Campers are sometimes allowed to collect water from the lodge and use the toilets and showers there, but this cannot always be relied upon. Be prepared to get supplies from Kalakol, or better still take everything you need (except fresh fish!) from Lodwar.
The lodge organises fishing trips and visits to Central Island or over to Alia Bay and Kubi Fora.

Make sure your tent is well pitched; strong winds often blow across Lake Turkana in the evenings, which can also make the lake surprisingly choppy at times.

MARALAL

Maralal is a small town in the foothills of the Samburu Highlands, a range of hills rising above the surrounding plains about halfway between the Mount Kenya massif and Lake Turkana.

This area is the homeland of the Samburu tribe, a semi-nomadic cattle rearing people related to the Maasai, and Maralal is their 'capital', with a colouful market, dukas, hotelis, a luxury lodge and a range of more basic B&Ls.

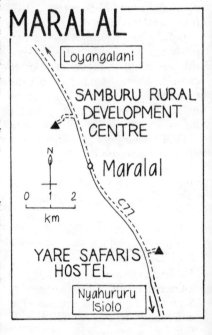

Maralal also boasts a purpose built hostel and campsite south of the town, and another site where camping is possible to the north.

Access
Car Maralal is 150 km north of Nyahururu (at the northern end of the Mount Kenya massif). The most direct route from Nyahururu is on the C77 road which eventually leads all the way to Loyangalani and North Horr. The road is tarred to Rumuruti, then graded dirt (rough in places) to Maralal.

Alternative routes, from Isiolo in the south-east and from Loruk (near Lake Baringo) in the south-west, both meeting the C77 south of Maralal, are scenically more interesting but tend to be used less frequently.

Bus/Hitch Usually one bus each day runs between Nyahururu and Maralal. Traffic on this route is light so hitching might take a long time. A bus also runs between Isiolo and Maralal, although this route would be very hard to hitch. The road from Loruk carries no public transport and is virtually impossible to hitch along.

YARE SAFARIS HOSTEL AND CAMPSITE

The Yare Safaris Hostel is a recognised Youth Hostel with a full time warden and staff. This is a well- positioned base for exploring Samburuland and other northern regions.

The hostel and campsite are in an area well outside the town in pleasant green hill-country. Zebra and gazelle roam freely but a strong fence protects campers from hyena and buffalo.

Bandas and dormitories are available and there is plenty of room for pitching a tent. Yare Safaris operate various trips and expeditions from the hostel, to the local area or further afield using 4WD vehicles or camels. Walking safaris are organised and guides are available for your own hiking or backpacking trips. A number of small lakes in the area make excellent destinations for a day's hike and offer good birdwatching.

IYHA members get a discount on dormitory accommodation and on all Yare-operated safaris.

Position   The hostel and campsite is well signposted about 4 km south of Maralal 200 m to the east of the C77 Nyahururu — Loyangalani road.

If you are coming into Maralal from the south get dropped here to avoid the walk back from the town.

Cost   30/— ppn. Tents for hire 40/— per night.

Facilities   Water, pit toilets, showers, firewood. Restaurant and lounge in hostel. Gear storage.

Security   Fence and askaris. One of the management is an important member of the local Samburu tribe so trouble is unlikely.

Bandas   470/- double.

Dormitories   70/-.

Transport   Yare safaris organise their own regular bus service between Nairobi and Maralal, free for IYHA members or people booked on a safari.

Enquiries   Mr Malcolm Gascoigne, Yare Safaris Ltd, PO Box 63006, Nairobi; Tel: 559313, or visit their office on the corner of Melili and Mukenia Roads, in Nairobi South C, a suburban area to the left (north-east) side of the main Mombasa road beyond the Nyayo Stadium (30 minutes walk from Kenyatta Ave).

THE ROAD TO EAST TURKANA

A single dirt track leads north from Maralal towards Loyangalani on the east shore of Lake Turkana. Unlike the road that leads up to Lodwar and the west shore, this eastern route is not tarred and so carries much less traffic.

Tourists in hired cars seldom attempt to drive from Maralal to the east shore due to the long distances involved and the difficult road conditions, especially in the short rainy season (April/May) when the track can be completely destroyed by flash-flood water. Most car-hire companies recommend their clients do not venture along this route, as petrol and spare part supplies are non-existent and assistance in the event of a mechanical breakdown extremely difficult to find. Only fully equipped vehicles (preferably travelling in convoy) with experienced drivers and competent mechanics should drive on these roads.

Public transport heading north from Maralal is rare, limited to the occasional matatu running up to Baragoi. Hitching may be possible in supply trucks, or with government and missionary vehicles. This may involve a day or two waiting, even longer further north, and payment might be expected.

A number of companies in Nairobi run camping safaris up to the east shore of Lake Turkana in specially built four-wheel-drive trucks, usually travelling via this Maralal — Loyangalani route. These safaris are the most reliable way of getting to Loyangalani, but drivers cannot pick up passengers along the route. Safaris can be arranged in Nairobi; details in the *Camping Safari Companies* section of this book.

For those intrepid drivers who can confidently set out from Maralal towards the north, the two main staging posts along this route are the small settlements of Baragoi and South Horr, both of which have campsites nearby.

BARAGOI CAMPSITE, Baragoi

Although it is the only major settlement in a very wide area Baragoi is still a one street town, with a two rows of Somali-owned dukas, some Samburu market stalls and hotelis, a church and a new police post.

The campsite is north of the town off the main track towards Loyangalani, but is not signposted. It is best to ask for directions at the police station. The site is often used by camping safari companies, but visits from independent campers are very unusual.

FOREST STATION, South Horr

Set amongst trees at the head of the relatively fertile Horr Valley and providing a welcoming break from the surrounding dry scrub-land, South Horr is a smaller place than Baragoi, with only one hoteli and duka on its single dusty main street.

The Forest Station, south of the main settlement, allows visitors to pitch tents on a sandy patch of ground outside the station compound.

Position   The Forest Station is signposted 1 km south of South Horr on the left (west) side of the main track coming in from Maralal.
Cost   3/– ppn.
Facilities   Tumbledown pit toilet. A nearby stream provides the only source of water for drinking and washing.
Security   Askari.

KURUNGU CAMP, Kurungu

Kurungu is north of South Horr, an official campsite organised by Safari Camp Services and used by them and other camping safari companies. The site is also open to individual travellers. The setting is pleasant, amongst shady trees, deep in the Horr Valley, but the local Samburu population have become very aware of tourists and sell trinkets or charge for photo poses. Dance shows are often arranged.
Position   Kurungu Camp is signposted 6 km north of South Horr on the right (east) side of the main track towards Loyangalani.
Cost   30/– ppn.
Facilities   Water, pit toilets, showers, firewood, fireplaces. Bandas are also available. During the main tourist season a small shop sells beer and sodas.
Enquiries   Safari Camp Services, PO Box 44801, Nairobi. Tel: 28936, 330130. (Office at corner of Koinange and Moktar Daddah Streets, Nairobi.)

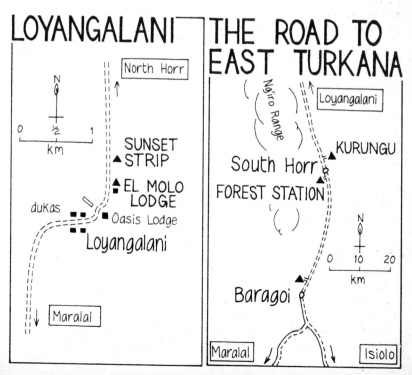

LOYANGALANI

Loyangalani lies at the southern end of Lake Turkana, and is the only settlement of any size on the east shore of the lake. For most travellers it marks the end of the long hot road up from Maralal that forces its way over scrubland, desert, and finally, lava fields, before dropping to the lake.

But despite the proximity of the waters of Lake Turkana, Loyangalani is still very much a desert town: hot, dry and dusty, especially when the infamous Turkana winds blow across the lake and onto the collection of mud walled dukas and houses that make up the settlement.

Loyangalani has one luxury lodge, catering mainly for fly-in guests and only open during the tourist season, two basic B&Ls, a few dukas and hotelis, and, to the north, two campsites.

Access

Loyangalani lies 200 km north of Maralal. The main route to Loyangalani from Maralal has been described above. Other routes to Loyangalani for self-contained vehicles or extremely dedicated hitchers are from Marsabit north of the Chalbi Desert via North Horr, or south of the desert and Mount Kulal via Kargi.

Tourists with vehicles should note that these northern routes are extremely serious, only to be attempted by fully-equipped cars, with experienced drivers and mechanics.

For travellers without vehicles there is absolutely no public transport on these routes to Loyangalani, except occasionally between Loyangalani and the settlements on the southern side of Mount Kulal. Transport from Marsabit is limited to supply lorries and missionary or government vehicles that, between them, may travel each road no more than two or three times per month.

No road transport of any kind links the western and eastern shores of Lake Turkana. The region directly south of the lake is extremely hostile desert and very sparsely populated. To travel from Lodwar to Loyangalani involves returning to Loruk, or more probably to Nakuru, before travelling north again on the Nyahururu – Maralal – Loyangalani route.

Fishing boats very rarely cross between the east and west shores of Lake Turkana, especially at the southern end of the lake.

EL MOLO LODGE

El Molo Lodge is a collection of fully furnished brick-built bandas surrounding a central bar and restaurant area. Although not specifically designed for camping, an area below the bandas has been set aside for tents. El Molo Lodge is only open during the tourist season.

Position El Molo Lodge is 1 km north of Loyangalani on the only track that leads out of town this way. The track passes between the Oasis

Lodge and the end of the airstrip. El Molo Lodge is clearly signposted on the right.
Cost   30/− ppn for camping.
Facilities   Water, toilets, showers. Swimming pool. Restaurant and bar.
Security   Askari and fence.
Bandas   300/− ppn.
Enquiries   El Molo Lodge, Tel: Nairobi 724384.

SUNSET STRIP

Sunset Strip consists of a line of bandas on a small sandy ridge looking across the wide shore of Lake Turkana towards the waters about 4 km away, and an area of sandy grass below the ridge for camping. True to its name, the campsite affords excellent views of the sunset, and for tents offers limited shelter from the winds amongst the palm trees.

Sunset Strip is organised by Safari Camp Services and often used by camping safari companies.

Position   1 km north of Loyangalani, 200 m beyond El Molo Lodge.
Cost   30/− ppn for camping.
Facilities   Water, good showers, pit toilets. Bar with shaded verandah (beer and sodas available in tourist season).
Security   Campsite staff, high fence.
Enquiries   Safari Camp Services, Nairobi. (See address in *The Road to East Turkana* above.)

The campsites at Loyangalani are often crowded and windswept. If you've got a vehicle carry on a few kilometres north towards El Molo Bay. A cliff by the lakeside makes a sheltered campsite. (A.R.

El Molo women, Lake Turkana.

MATHEWS RANGE

The Mathews Range is a group of hills and mountains stretching north from the plains above Samburu National Reserve as far as the Ndoto Mountains. The range's African name is Ol Doinyo Lenkyio. Although the surrounding plains are dry most of the year the hills of the Mathews Range are high enough to form clouds, and the resulting rains provide streams and lush forest that support a great variety of wildlife. At the southern end of the range the Nyeng River flows through the little visited Kitich Valley.

Kitich Camp, a luxury tented camp, has been established by the river in the Kitich Valley, and the area's endangered herd of black rhino are guarded by a Wildlife Department team based in the valley supported by the African Fund for Endangered Wildlife.

KITICH VALLEY PUBLIC CAMPSITE

The Wildlife Department have a public campsite near their control centre in the southern part of the Kitich Valley. The site is situated on cleared ground near the river. Fully equipped campers are welcome, but must reserve the site before arrival with Let's Go Travel, Nairobi.

Position   Kitich Public Campsite lies north of the small town of Wamba, which is situated near the junction of the C78/C79 Maralal – Archer's Post road (graded) and the minor dirt track to Barsaloi (sometimes spelt Parsaloi). Wamba is 70 km from Archer's Post by road. Beyond Wamba routes are difficult to follow but Let's Go Travel provide maps and directions.
Cost   30/– ppn.
Facilities   Water, toilet. Guides for game-walks can be arranged at Kitich Camp reception. (Campers are not permitted to use other Kitich Camp facilities). Basic supplies in Wamba or Archer's Post.
Security   Theft is unlikely, but askaris can be hired if required.
Bookings/Enquiries   For further details about the exclusive Kitich Camp or the Kitich Valley Public Campsite contact Let's Go Travel, Standard Street, Nairobi.

The Mathews Range offers endless wild camping opportunities for fully equipped intrepid backpackers. The range is seldom visited by tourists, and the local people unused to foreigners. Only experienced campers familiar with bush-walking should consider setting out on major expeditions through the range. The public campsite at Kitich Valley makes a good base to start from.

Gerhard Bronner (West Germany) sent this tale about his wild camping in the Mathews Range.

When we left the forested ridge and forced our way through dense bush Simon, my Samburu guide, found wild bees in a hollow tree. He chased them away with smoke and then removed the honey. I tried a bit, but Simon and the two boys, Paulo and Raymon, took huge bites of the cone eating honey and larvae. After chewing and sucking they spat out the wax.

Then we descended to the foot of the slope. There was a clear, cool river, just the right thing after being soaked with sweat after crossing the mountains. After a refreshing bath we looked for a place to spend the night. There was a small platform, bordered by the river on one side and a rock on the other. We considered it quite safe from wild animals, the most likely being hyenas. I pitched my tent, and the three Samburus slept outside. That night I suffered a lot from small biting flies.

The next day we set out across the plains. Simon heard a honey-bird and he and Raymon followed it to find the honey. Paulo and I continued alone. I felt a bit worried without Simon, knowing there was plenty of wildlife around.

We passed a hill and left the grassland into woodland. We couldn't see very far and just kept to the direction where I knew there was a river. Suddenly I saw a movement and just glimpsed an animal's back and tail about fifty metres away. Paulo saw it too. It was definitely no gazelle so we rushed to some trees and climbed to a safe height. Then Paulo said he saw it again, and it was a male lion. The lion moved away and after making some noise without any reaction we descended and went carefully on.

When we reached the river with its denser vegetation we followed it back towards the campsite, always prepared to run for a tree in case we met any of the buffalo that came to drink here. Suddenly we heard some trampling on the road ahead of us. We didn't know whether it was a buffalo or an elephant but I shouted to Paulo, dropped my rucksack and ran back. Paulo ran, fell, but stood up quickly and continued. We both rushed to the same tree and, climbing, got some scratches. We waited for a while then went down when nothing happened. Probably it was an elephant that fled when it noticed our coming.

Finally we reached the campsite. After a while the other two arrived telling us that they saw a lion as well, and also several elephants. During the night the flies were busy again covering the parts of my skin they had missed last night with itching spots.

The following day we went back to the other side of the mountains, but didn't have any more encounters with the wildlife.

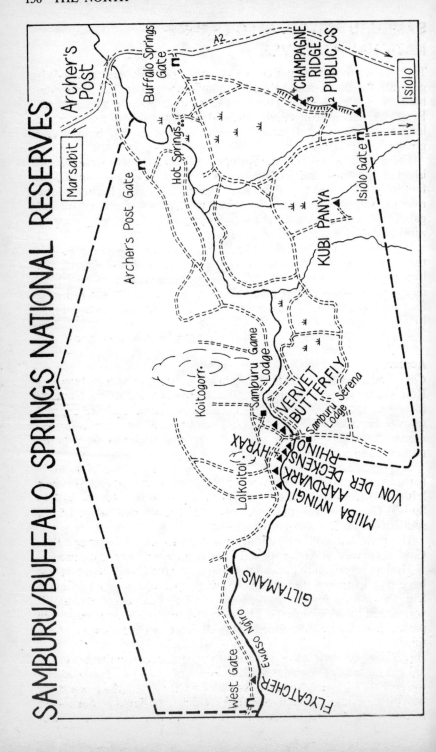

SAMBURU AND BUFFALO SPRINGS NATIONAL RESERVES

The area north of Mount Kenya and east of the Samburu highlands is generally dry bushland inhabited by nomadic tribespeople and only the hardiest of wild animals. Through this region flows the Ewaso Ngiro River, a source of constant water, and on either side of the river are large tracts of grassland, turned to brown most of the year but rich and green after the rains.

The Samburu and Buffalo Springs National Reserves were established on the north and south banks of the Ewaso Ngiro to protect the fine selection of wildlife that inhabits this grassland and relies on the river for water. Leopard is often sighted here, as are oryx, elephant and gazelle, plus more unusual species such as reticulated giraffe, Grevy's zebra and the blue-legged Somali ostrich.

It was necessary to establish two reserves because the Ewaso Ngiro is the boundary between two district councils, so each reserve is controlled by a different council. Direction signs in the reserves are non-existent in many places, although major features and campsites can usually be found. Tracks around the reserves are generally good, and can be used by 2WD vehicles in the dry season.

Standard national reserve entrance fees are payable at all gates.

Access
Car   The most direct route to Samburu and Buffalo Springs National Reserves from Nairobi is on the main A2 road via Thika and Nanyuki (or round the east side of Mount Kenya via Embu and Meru), and through Isiolo. From Nairobi to Isiolo is about 300 km on good tarred road. After Isiolo the A2 road goes all the way to Moyale but is badly potholed and corrugated in many places.

Buffalo Springs National Reserve can be reached via: Isiolo Gate (called Gare Mara Gate on some maps) on a graded road that branches left (west) from the A2 about 20 km north of Isiolo; or via Buffalo Springs Gate, also west of the A2, about 30 km north of Isiolo, 3.5 km south of the small town of Archer's Post.

The main entrance to Samburu National Reserve is Archer's Post Gate, 5 km west of Archer's Post. The West Gate is very rarely used.

The two reserves are joined by a bridge over the Ewaso Ngiro. If you have paid entrance into Buffalo Springs, you are allowed to enter Samburu for the day but must pay entrance and camping/lodge fees if you intend to stay longer. At present this restriction does not apply passing from Samburu to Buffalo Springs, but may be introduced at any time.

Bus/Hitch   Regular buses and matatus run to Isiolo from all the towns around the central highlands. From Isiolo one bus per day heads up towards the remote northern towns via Archer's Post, which offers the best possibilities for travellers with no vehicles. It should be possible to hitch this far. At Archer's Post you can wait by the track to the gate or walk to the gate and wait for a lift there. Official park vehicles run between Archer's Post and Samburu Lodge twice per day. You may find a lift round the park at the campsites or at the lodge. If all else fails, the lodge runs daily game drives for 240/− per person.

CAMPING, Samburu
Samburu has a string of eight campsites spread along the north bank of the Ewaso Ngiro River between Samburu Lodge and the West Gate. All are flat cleared spaces under trees.

The difference between special and public campsites that exists in other parks and reserves is not distinct here; some public sites have no facilities, while some of the special sites have limited facilities and are open to the public. The warden advises using the sites nearer the lodge and park offices as these tend to be more secure.

Cost 30/− ppn. Special campsites 300/− psw.
Booking The Warden, Samburu National Reserve, PO Box 27, Isiolo.

Vervet Special Campsite
This site is the nearest to the lodge, and popular with camping safari companies.
Facilities The single pit toilet is dirty and bat-infested. Water must be collected from the nearby workers' houses.
Security Theft by humans is not unknown, and campers are also pestered by frighteningly large baboons.

Butterfly Public Campsite
Very near Vervet Campsite in a similar postion. A single toilet is the only facility.

During daylight hours it is possible to walk from Butterfly or Vervet Campsites to the lodge for a cold drink and a look at the crocs. This is not advised after 1900 h when the lodge gates are locked and the nightly leopard bait is laid.

At Samburu Lodge there's a terrace overlooking the river flowing between sandy banks, and on these sandy banks a couple of huge crocodiles lounge waiting for their next gift of baited meat. All very well if you're in a nice snug lodge, but near the campsite where we were staying was another sandy bank, just like the one by the lodge. OK, there was nothing on it this time, but I'm sure one sandy bank is very much like another to a crocodile, and there was plenty of fresh meat, in the form of campers, in the vacinity…!

The moral of the tale: Make sure all campers know that there are crocs in the river here. (Elizabeth Slinn, Nairobi)

All other campsites have no facilities:
Rhino Public Campsite,
Von Der Deckens Special Campsite,
Hyrax Public Campsite,
Aardvark Special Campsite – reserved for large parties,
Miiba Nyingi Special Campsite – regarded as the prettiest site,
Giltamans Special Campsite,
Flycatcher Special Campsite.

When we camped at Samburu, during early June, the weather was cool and breezy and the park was in excellent condition with green grass and plenty of wildlife to be seen. This is not always the case and campers should bring mosquito nets. The breeze cannot always be relied on to keep the mosquitoes off. (Linda Brown, NY, USA)

CAMPING, Buffalo Springs
Cost   30/– ppn.

Champagne Ridge Public Campsites
None of the public campsites spread along Champagne Ridge have any facilities and are used so infrequently that they have become overgrown and difficult to find. At present campers are advised not to use these sites as robberies have occured in the past.

Kubi Panya Special Campsite
This site is in the southern area of the reserve on the west bank of the Maji Ya Chumvi River. The site has no facilities and is seldom used.

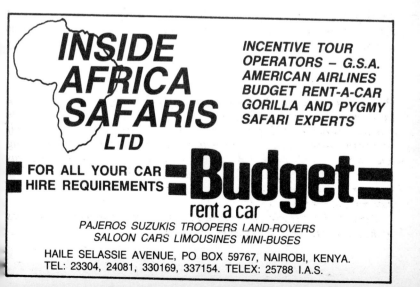

MARSABIT NATIONAL PARK

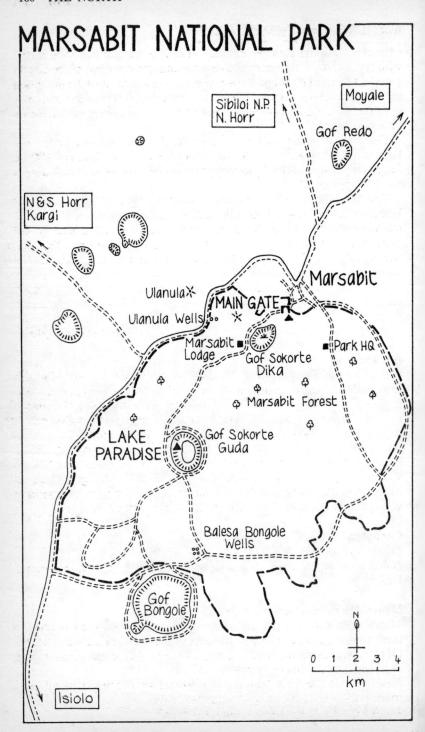

Moyale

Sibiloi N.P.
N. Horr

Gof Redo

N&S Horr
Kargi

Ulanula

Ulanula Wells

MAIN GATE

Marsabit

Marsabit
Lodge

Gof Sokorte
Dika

Park HQ

Marsabit Forest

LAKE
PARADISE

Gof Sokorte
Guda

Balesa Bongole
Wells

Gof
Bongole

N

0 1 2 3 4
km

Isiolo

MARSABIT NATIONAL PARK

Marsabit National Reserve consists of a huge extinct volcano, dotted with small craters, that rises above the south-eastern edge of the Chalbi Desert. Marsabit National Park covers the highest parts of the mountain at the centre of the reserve. Hot air from the desert cools and condenses over the mountain forming mist and rain which supports vast stretches of dense forest.

The park is particularly renowned for elephant, greater kudu, and large numbers of buffalo. Giraffe, zebra, leopard and lion can also be seen, but because of the dense vegetation wildlife can be difficult to spot away from water holes.

The best place for viewing animals is at the largest of the craters, Gof Bongole, as the vegetation thins and the gof is circled by a drivable track. Other recommended viewing spots are the seasonal lake in Gof Sokorte Dika near the lodge, or at Lake Paradise. Visitors to Marsabit will also see a wide variety of birds, and may come across some of the mountain's large population of snakes as well!

Due to its isolated locality, Marsabit is not a busy park, and many campers find they have the campsites, and the park, completely to themselves.

Standard national park entrance fees are payable at the main gate.

Access

Car The main approach to Marsabit National Park is via Marsabit town which lies at the centre of the national reserve on the main A2 road between Isiolo and Moyale, about 280 km north of Isiolo. The road is graded and drivable for all vehicles, but badly corrugated in places. The main entrance into the park is the gate to the south of the town.

Bus/Hitch A bus runs between Isiolo and Moyale via Marsabit three times per week in each direction. Hitching is also possible on this road with occasional supply trucks and government vehicles. Once at Marsabit walkers are not allowed into the park, but travellers without vehicles have often hitched a ride to the lodge with the rangers.

CAMPING

Cost 30/− ppn. Special campsites 300/− psw.

Booking The Warden, Marsabit National Park, PO Marsabit, via Isiolo.

Main Gate Public Campsite (No 2)

Marsabit used to have two public sites, but Public Campsite No 1 on the track towards the park HQ to the east of the main gate is now closed. Only Public Campsite No 2 is open, but even this seems to be seldom used and is becoming overgrown.

Position On the track between Marsabit town and the main entrance to the park, about 200 m before the park gate.

Facilities Water from gate, toilet, firewood.

Lake Paradise Special Campsite

Many campers have reported staying here without needing to reserve in advance or pay the reservation fee, even though it is a special campsite, as visitors are rare.

Position   Lake Paradise is in the Gof Sokorte Guda crater, and the campsite is on its western edge.

Facilities   None.

At 2000 m Marsabit Mountain gets very cold at night. I camped by Lake Paradise which was beautiful, although nights were chilly, and the lake is shrouded in mist early in the mornings. But it usually clears about mid-day. (John Kerrin, Australia)

SIBILOI NATIONAL PARK

Sibiloi, formerly known as East Rudolf National Park, lies on the eastern shore of Lake Turkana in the far north of Kenya, only 30 km from the border with Ethiopia. The park was originally created to protect the area of Kubi Fora, where a *Homo habilis* skull, and numerous other bones and tools dating from prehistoric times, were first discovered in 1972.

Excavation continues sporadically at Kubi Fora and the site is open to visitors for viewing, but visitors to the Sibiloi National Park are often surprised to learn that this area also contains a varied selection of wildlife. Zebra, hartebeest and topi are common, while lion and even cheetah can be spotted on occasions.

The landscape is not unlike the area of the rift valley north of Lake Baringo, with small rocky outcrops and dry river beds, but with more apparent wildlife. Animals drink from the lake or browse on the trees growing in the dry river beds. This area is not inhabited by people, only fishermen on the lake are occasionally seen.

Standard national parks entrance fees are payable at Alia Bay park headquarters. (Just because Sibiloi seems at the end of the world, it doesn't mean you don't have to pay!)

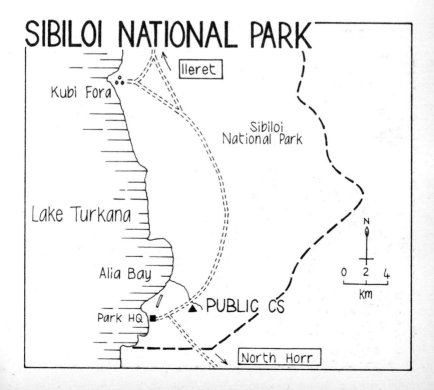

Access

Car   Sibiloi is very remote. The roads to the park are bad even by northern standards and only fully equipped expedition vehicles should attempt to drive there. The two main routes to the park headquarters at Alia Bay are from Loyangalani, and from Marsabit. The track from Marsabit is regarded as the better of the two (or the least bad) and drivers on both routes tend to go through North Horr. Guides can be hired in Loyangalani.

Hitching   No public transport of any kind runs to Sibiloi, but occasional supply vehicles do make the journey between Marsabit and the park, and intrepid hitchers have managed to get rides to Alia Bay and even right up to Ileret. A national park vehicle based at Alia Bay comes to Marsabit at the end of the month, stays for about a week, then returns to Alia Bay. A police vehicle from Ileret comes to Marsabit for supplies, also at the end of every month, but returns to Ileret after only a few days. For information about these vehicles ask at the National Park HQ or the police station in Marsabit. No more than two or three vehicles of any sort travel these roads each month. On the road between Loyangalani and Alia Bay there's even less. If you do hitch to Sibiloi be prepared for a long wait to get back, too!

Plane   For travellers not on a tight budget or without the luxury of unlimited time it is posible to fly to Alia Bay. Many visitors fly to the park from the lodges at Loyangalani or Ferguson's Gulf.

CAMPING

Alia Bay is Sibiloi Park's HQ with some official buildings, an airstrip, and a campsite. The campsite is beside a dry river bed about 4 km from the airstrip.

El Molo girl, Lake Turkana.

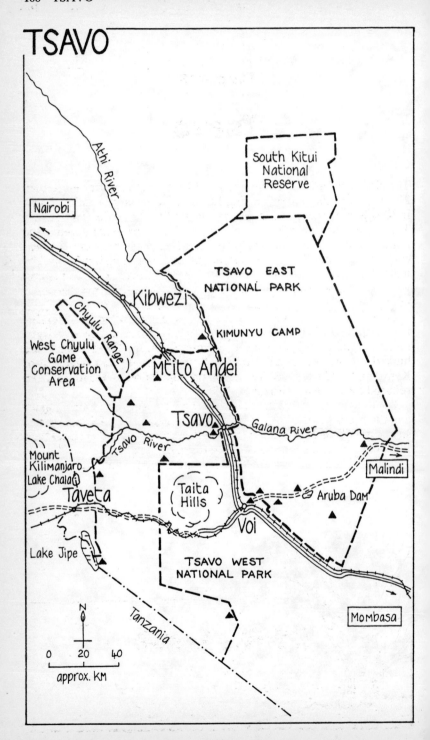

TSAVO

South Kitui National Reserve

Athi River

Nairobi

TSAVO EAST NATIONAL PARK

Kibwezi

KIMUNYU CAMP

Chyulu Range

West Chyulu Game Conservation Area

Mtito Andei

Tsavo

Galana River

Mount Kilimanjaro
Lake Chala

Tsavo River

Taveta

Taita Hills

Malindi

Aruba Dam

Voi

Lake Jipe

TSAVO WEST NATIONAL PARK

Tanzania

Mombasa

N

0   20   40

approx. KM

Chapter 13

Tsavo

The National Parks of Tsavo West and East together cover more than 21,000 square kilometres, making Tsavo by far the largest national park in Kenya and among the largest in the world. The parks (particularly Tsavo West) are included in many tourists' safari plans, but even in the popular areas, the available space means visitors and game are less concentrated, and less obvious, than in other more popular parks. For many visitors the main attraction of Tsavo is the experience of space; vast landscapes, huge African skies, and a lasting impression of untouched emptiness.

Like many other national parks in Kenya, Tsavo suffers considerably from elephant and rhino poaching, but due to its size and the scarcity of resources the park is difficult to patrol efficiently. These animals are hunted for their tusks and horns, which are usually smuggled out of Kenya and sold overseas. The elephant population in Tsavo has been reduced by over two thirds since 1981.

Roads in the parks are generally good in all weathers as traffic is light, and the roads themselves have a natural murram base. Directions and signposts are usually clear in the well used areas of the parks, and junctions are marked by big numbered stones.

Standard national park entrance fees are payable at all gates.

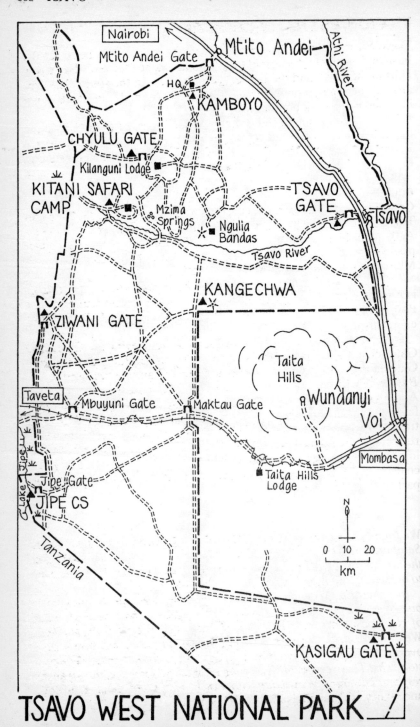

TSAVO WEST NATIONAL PARK

TSAVO WEST NATIONAL PARK

Tsavo West National Park covers over 7,000 square kilometres of dry bushland mostly to the west of the Mombasa Road, between the Chyulu Hills in the north and the border with Tanzania in the south. The area around the highly populated and intensively farmed Taita Hills is not included in the park boundaries.

Visitors who come to see game will spend most of their time in the higher and better watered Ngulia area of the park, north of the Tsavo River. Those who come to experience Tsavo's empty grandeur will find the south of the park rarely visited.

Access

Car The two main entrances into the park are Mtito Andei Gate and Tsavo Gate about 230 and 280 km south-east of Nairobi on the main A109 Nairobi — Mombasa road. The A23 Voi — Taveta road which passes through the central section of the park via Maktau Gate and Mbuyuni Gate is tarred between Voi and Bura.

Chyulu Gate (also spelt Kyulu), in the north-west corner of the park, is used by vehicles coming into Tsavo West from Amboseli National Park. Four wheel drive and high clearance is advisable for this route, especially in wet weather.

Other entry points are at: Ziwani Gate, north of Mbuyuni Gate; Jipe Gate, near Lake Jipe on the south-west border of the park; Kasigau Gate, in the south-east. These are more remote and seldom used.

Bus/Hitch Buses between Nairobi and Mombasa pass near Mtito Andei Gate and Tsavo River Gate. Hitching to these gates would be fairly easy, but as walking is not generally allowed inside the park, travellers without vehicles may have a very long wait here. Buses also run between Voi and Taveta on the Tanzania border, or even to Moshi in Tanzania, through the park via Maktau and Mbuyuni Gates. The chances of seeing game from the bus, or getting a lift further into the park at the gates, are slight.

We found the southern part of Tsavo West as remote as the semi-desert Samburu lands around North Horr. When we camp we enjoy looking at the birdlife so do not like interruptions. It was as if we had the whole park to ourselves, so for us Tsavo is an excellent place.

In Tsavo East, though, we did not have the campsite at Voi gate to ourselves. We were completely surprised by the unexpected appearance of elephants at the waterhole only about twenty metres from our tent. We'd heard a rumbling which sounded like a motorbike being kicked over in Voi town, and ignored it. This was the sound of the elephants' stomachs! They seemed fairly unconcerned at our presence, but we kept a respectful distance. We will not ignore such sounds next time! (Ben Rode and Nancy O'Donnell, Nairobi and USA)

CAMPING
Cost   30/− ppn. Special campsites 1000/− psw.
Booking   The Warden, Tsavo West National Park, PO Mtito Andei.

Mtito Andei Gate
The original campsite inside the gate is now closed. Latecomers would be allowed to camp at the gate for one night.
Facilities   Water, pit toilet.
Security   No askari, rangers nearby.

Kamboyo Campsite
Position   8 km from Mtito Andei near the Park HQ.
Facilities   Water, pit toilet.

Chyulu Gate/Kilanguni Public Campsite
This used to be a very good site, but the grass is wearing thin and rubbish is piling up as it becomes over-used by budget safari companies. Baboons can be a problem.
Position   Inside the national park boundary just outside Chyulu Gate.
Facilities   Water, toilets, showers, firewood, shelters for shade.
Game viewing is possible by the floodlit waterhole and saltlick at the nearby Kilanguni Lodge. The lodge is beyond the park gate so you should 'make arrangements' to overcome the rule forbidding driving after 1900 h.

Kitani Safari Camp Special Campsites
These two sites west of Kitani Safari Camp are for experienced campers used to Tsavo. You need to be completely self-sufficient (include a panga for clearing the grass), and aware that the area can be full of game.
   Bandas are available at Kitani Safari Camp and at the nearby Ngulia Safari Camp. Both include mosquito nets and well maintained cookers. Pay at the bandas. Cost: 168/−.

Ziwani Gate Public Campsite
This site is remote and has no facilities. The bandas outside the gate are nicely sited and cost 30/− ppn). Take all your own food and water.

Jipe Public Campsite
Position   On the lower eastern shore of Lake Jipe in the south-western corner of the park, a grassy lakeside site offering excellent views of the North Pare Mountains and Mount Kilimanjaro in Tanzania.
Facilities   Water, toilets, showers, fireplaces. Bandas. Boats for hire. Beers and other luxuries available from the new Lake Jipe Lodge.
Warning   Water for both drinking and showers is pumped directly from the lake which is not free of bilharzia. Hippos graze at night, as will lake flies and mosquitoes if your nets are inadequate.

Kasigau Gate
This campsite has no facilities, and is rarely used. There are rumoured to be ruby mines in this area.

Tsavo Gate Public Campsite
Position   In the north-east of the park, near where the main Nairobi −
Mombasa road crosses the Tsavo River, 4 km from the gate.
Facilities   None. Collect water from the gate.
The looming presence of a string of electricity pylons detracts from the remoteness.

Kangechwa Special Campsite
Position   Near a small hill of the same name in the central area of the park between the Taita and the Ngulia Hills. Very remote, no facilities.

Near Kitani Safari Camp are **Mzima Springs**, large pools of clear water where it's possible to see hippos and crocodiles from a specially constructed underwater view point.

Near Ziwani Campsite, but outside the park boundary, is **Lake Chala**, a remote, blue crater lake on the Tanzania border. It is a surprising four hour walk around the crater. Swimming is possible, crocodiles permitting. People have camped at the crater rim, but there may be a slight security risk so a group would be advisable. Easiest access is from the main Voi − Taveta road. A drivable track leads from a junction with this road about 3 km east of Taveta town to Lake Chala. 4WD is needed to drive to the top of the crater.

Between Lakes Jipe and Chala is **Grogan's Castle**, a ruined Hollywood-style 'folly' on a single knoll rising above the surrounding sisal estates. An askari will show you around for 20/−, and tell you the story.

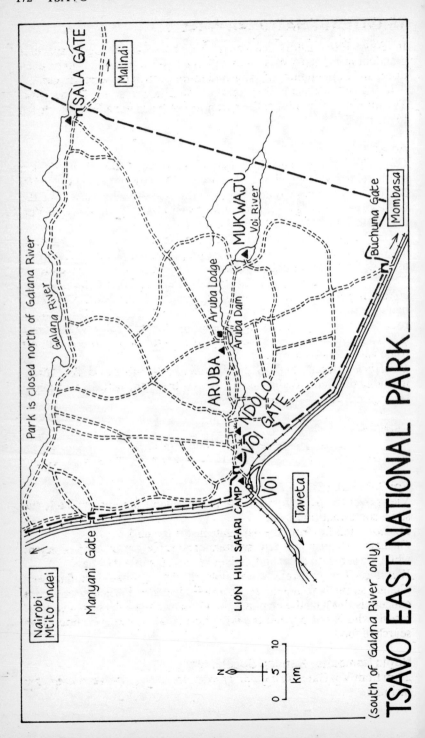

TSAVO EAST NATIONAL PARK

(south of Galana River only)

TSAVO EAST NATIONAL PARK

In Tsavo East visitors can experience the same feeling of spacious grandeur as in Tsavo West, although the eastern park tends to be even drier, and even emptier of game and tourists, than the western park.

In Tsavo East game is generally found in the south of the park. Two-thirds of Tsavo East, the part north of the Galana River, is closed to the public.

Access

Car   The main entrance into Tsavo East is Voi Gate, about 320 km south-east of Nairobi, about 5 km north of Voi town on the main A109 Nairobi – Mombasa road. Other entrances into the park from the Naorobi – Mombasa road are at Manyani Gate, 25 km north of Voi, and at Buchuma Gate 45 km to the south-east.

The gate at Mtito Andei into Tsavo East is, in effect, a private gate to Tsavo Tented Safari Camp (a tented lodge) and to Kimunyu Campsite as roads from here into the southern part of the park are impassable.

It is also possible to enter the park on the road from Malindi (on the coast) via Sala Gate on the eastern boundary of the park. This route is badly rutted in parts and can be difficult in the rains. Note also that the route alongside the Galana River between Manyani Gate and Sala Gate is often impassable due to flooding. It is better to use the less direct route via Aruba Dam.

Bus/Hitch   Buses run between Nairobi and Mombasa via Voi. Hitching along this main road is fine but people travelling without cars would be very lucky to find a lift at any of the gates.

CAMPING

Cost   30/– ppn. Special campsites 1000/– psw.
Booking   The Warden, Tsavo East National Park, PO Box 14, Voi.

Voi Gate Public Campsites

Views over the park from the site are excellent, but unfortunately the site is somewhat rundown.
Position   0.5 km from the park gate inside the park.
Facilities   Bandas and tent shelters are usable but in need of repair while the concrete toilet and shower block is inhabited by bats.
Warning   The concrete water hole attracts animals including elephants, so pitch your tent at a sensible distance. Particular cause for concern is Buknazi the elephant, hand-reared as a baby now a teenage rascal, who is not beyond breaking into bandas, and even houses, in search of food.

Ndolo Campsite / Kanderi Special Site

2 km from Voi Gate, *'in a spooky forest, near a bug infested swamp'*. No facilities.

Aruba Campsite

Position In the centre of the southern section of Tsavo East near Aruba Dam.

Facilities Water, dirty pit toilets. Canteen, shop with cool beers and limited food supplies.

Bandas 168/− ppn.

Aruba Lodge has no petrol, and water is taken in by tanker at present. The nearby Aruba Dam is inhabited by a solitary hippo and attracts game and birds during the dry season which can be seen from the lodge. The dam also attracts mosquitoes.

Mukwaju Special Campsite

This site is only for adventurers. It is in an isolated position, about 15 km to the east of Aruba, and has no facilities. It is excellent for reclusive campers, although huge electricity pylons spoil the southern view with reminders of civilisation.

Sala Gate Public Campsite

This site is often used by safari companies operating from Malindi or the coast so can become crowded in the tourist seasons. No facilities.

Masalini (Bushwhackers) Campsite, east of Kibwezi, is now closed.

Crocodile Tented Camp, outside the park, 15 km beyond Sala gate towards Malindi, is not open to the public for camping.

Kimunyu Campsite

A privately owned camping area is planned near Tsavo Tented Safari Camp, on the banks of the Athi River, which forms the eastern boundary of Tsavo East National Park. The camping area will consist of seven sites; three on the Athi River and three on the nearby Kimunyu River (each with space for four tents plus vehicles), and a special large site for overland trucks. As this book goes to press Kimunyu Campsite has not been completed.

Position Kimunyu Campsite is 16 km east of Mtito Andei Gate (East) and is reached via the dirt road to the Tented Safari Camp.

Enquiries Mr Lionel Nutter, PO Box 6, Mtito Andei.

Near the Voi Gate entrance to the park is the compound home of **Eleanor** the famous orphaned elephant, who is now grown up and adopts orphans herself. The whole family can sometimes be seen out on the plains beyond Voi Gate or daily at dusk feeding in their compound.

TSAVO AREA

Two other campsites exist in the Tsavo area, but are outside the boundaries of the national parks.

RIVERSIDE CAMPSITE, Tsavo

Position   Just south of the the main A109 Nairobi − Mombasa road where it crosses the Tsavo River, just south of the Tsavo Gate entrance into Tsavo West National Park.

Cost   30/− ppn.

Facilities   Water from the river (beware of crocodiles), very basic toilet. There are plans to develop bandas.

Further downstream better sites can be found, however these have no facilities at all and are technically inside the park.

The nearby Maneaters Motel (two lions terrorised navvies working on the construction of the railway at the beginning of the century) has no accommodation, only petrol pumps, a cafeteria and an expensive shop.

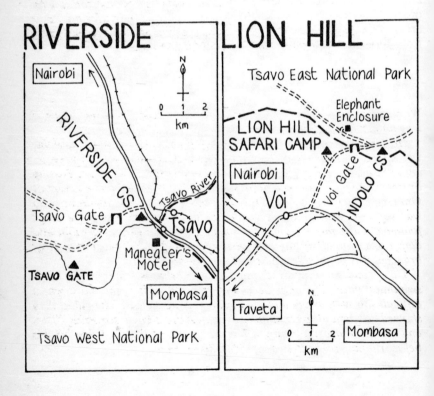

LION HILL SAFARI CAMP, Voi

A newly established camp, with bandas, a small bar and restaurant, and a field for camping. The site is well maintained, and has a good atmosphere.

Position   Situated about 4 km north-west of Voi town, on the left side of the main track to the Voi Gate entrance into Tsavo East National Park.

Cost   30/-ppn.

Facilities   Water, toilets, showers. Evening meals by arrangement. The camp is lit by kerosene lamps at present, but should have electricity in 1989.

Security   Fence and askari.

Address   PO Box 298, Voi. Tel: Voi 2647.

Warning   The size and remoteness of the Tsavo parks is an attraction for tourists, but also makes the parks a paradise for poachers. As the elephant population suffers severe reductions the government of Kenya has become aware of the problem and is increasingly concerned. In an attempt to combat the poachers armed rangers patrol the parks with orders to shoot suspects on sight. Tourists visiting the parks may find areas of the parks closed, and should not get out of their vehicles away from designated campsites and official viewing points.

We camped at Voi Gate and met an American researcher based in Tsavo who told some good stories about the animals in this area.

Most of the stories we hear about Tsavo involve the elephants, and this was no exception. One of Eleanor's adopted orphans was growing up and, like all youngsters, was going through an inquisitive phase. Passing by one of the park workers' houses this elephant decided that a packet of Omo might be worth eating. This news was carried to the researcher who was very worried, and had visions of this elephant eating the soap, foaming at the mouth, and being shot by the rangers as a rabid and dangerous animal! Fortunately the elephant decided that the taste of branches was preferable, and came to no harm.

The second story involved one of Tsavo's rhinos falling into a lodge swimming pool. The poor beast was frenzied with fright and it was a difficult job with slings and a lorry to pull him clear. The rhino then showed his gratitude by trampling over most of the lawn, scattering chairs and tables, and demolishing a bar and some of the pool-side bandas before running off back to a more familiar habitat.

THE COAST

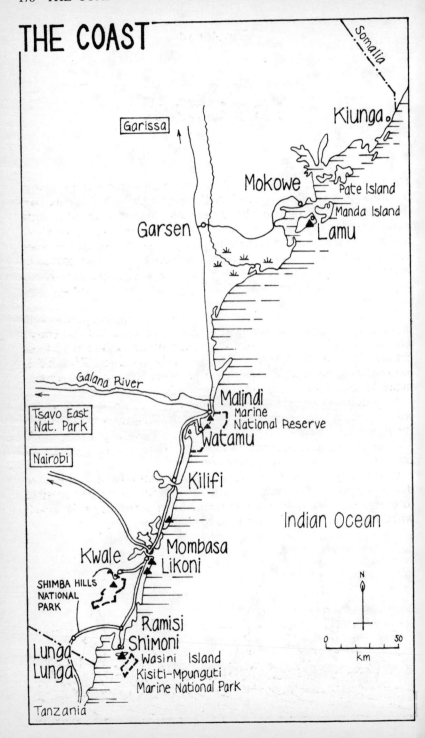

Chapter 14

The Coast

The first visitors to the coast of Kenya were explorers and merchants from the Arab kingdoms around the Persian Gulf who had sailed down the East African shoreline from a time long before historical records were kept. They established commercial centres and later great cities, trading with the Bantu tribes from the interior and also with the peoples of India and Asia who crossed the ocean every year with the monsoon winds. As business links became stronger Arab and Bantu intermarried, and over the centuries a completely separate Swahili culture was established.

The people of the coast are still called Swahili today and their language, Kiswahili, has become the common tongue of East Africa. The Swahili still look to Arabia rather than Africa as the root of their culture; Islam is the dominant religion on the coast and Kiswahili is loosely based on Arabic, although it has since developed to contain many African, Portuguese and English words.

In modern times the Indian Ocean coastline has become very popular with European package tourists who come to Kenya for the clear sea, the clean sand, and two weeks of guaranteed sun. Every year new hotels and beach-clubs are wedged in between private holiday villas and cottages.

If you fancy a bit of resort life, a few campsites remain on the more developed parts of the coast, but with a tent, of course, it is also possible to escape completely to enjoy the palm-lined pleasures of the beach without a single block of concrete to spoil the view.

MOMBASA

Mombasa has been a Swahili citadel, a Portuguese fortress, and a strategic port for the British Empire into the colonies of East Africa. Today Mombasa is an important commercial centre, Kenya's second city and one of the largest ports on the East African coastline. There are refineries and factories on the outskirts of the city, but the narrow streets and alleys of the Old Town still retain much of their traditional atmosphere.

Access

Car   The main A109 Nairobi – Mombasa road is tarred all the way and the 500 km can be covered in five to six hours' steady driving. The road can be quite busy at times, mainly with heavy trucks coming from Mombasa docks heading towards Nairobi or the landlocked countries of Central Africa. Driving standards are often appalling. A break or two on the way gives you a chance to rest and helps your concentration.

Bus/Hitch   There are regular daily and nightly bus services between Nairobi and Mombasa. Hitching is no problem and unless you get a lift in a very slow truck you should be able to do it in one day.

Train   A safe and reasonably priced alternative to travelling by road between Nairobi and Mombasa. Clean, comfortable, and rarely more than a couple of hours late. For times and reservations ask at the station or at a travel agent.

Plane   Visitors short on time may choose to fly between Nairobi and Mombasa. Kenya Airways operate several flights each day.

Mombasa has hotels for all budgets, but no camping is allowed anywhere in the city. The nearest campsites are to the south of the city at Likoni.

YWCA, Likoni

The YWCA has a large hostel in Mombasa, and this small hostel and campsite at Likoni, a five minute ferry ride across the harbour entrance, close enough for daily visits into the city. The position is breezy and provides good views across to Mombasa. Camping is by the car park on grass beneath trees. The staff are friendly and allow bags to be stored in the office during the day.

Position   The Likoni Ferry is south of Mombasa city centre on the main A14 road to the south. From the ferry go up the hill and take the first turning on the left (200 m). The YWCA is on the left after 100 m.

Cost   20/– ppn.

Facilities   Water, toilets, showers and a veranda sitting area are provided by the hostel. Open fires are allowed with permission, but no wood is provided.

TIBWANI BEACH, Tibwani

This is a field only, about 4 km south of the ferry along the narrow coast road, just past the sign for 'Childrens Holiday Resort' on the left. Camping is free, but the site has no facilities except being right by the beach. A duka opposite provides some basics but there's absolutely no security in an area where theft from tourists is common. Camping here cannot be recommended at all.

On the main road ignore signs 3 km south of the Likoni Ferry to 'Farahs Camping'. This has long since closed, but the locals will happily guide you from sign to sign until you realise that these are all that remain.

For campsites further south than Likoni, see the *South of Mombasa* section.

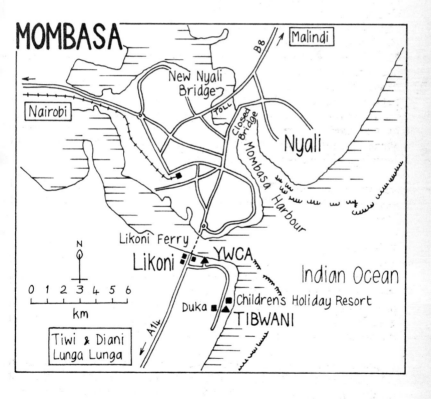

NORTH OF MOMBASA

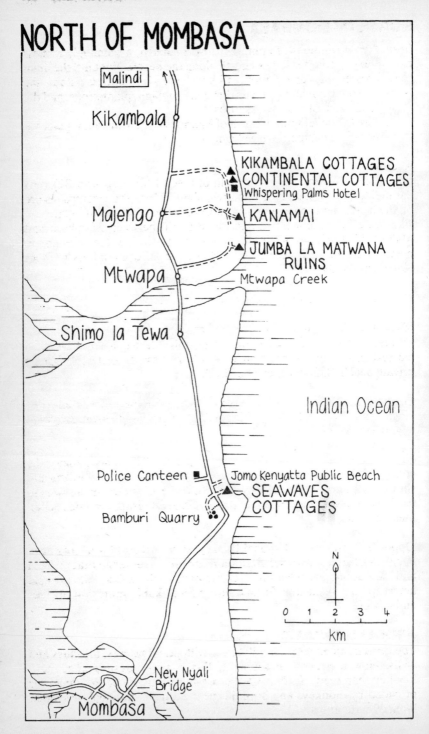

Malindi

Kikambala

KIKAMBALA COTTAGES
CONTINENTAL COTTAGES
Whispering Palms Hotel

Majengo

KANAMAI

JUMBA LA MATWANA
RUINS

Mtwapa

Mtwapa Creek

Shimo la Tewa

Indian Ocean

Police Canteen

Jomo Kenyatta Public Beach
SEAWAVES
COTTAGES

Bamburi Quarry

N

0   1   2   3   4
km

New Nyali
Bridge

Mombasa

NORTH OF MOMBASA

From Nyali, Mombasa's upmarket resort suburb, a seemingly endless row of luxury hotels stretches north along the beach. Not until the main road crosses Mtwapa Creek, 18 km beyond Mombasa, does the landscape open out and you pass through farmland, plantations, and the occasional patch of indigenous forest.

Despite the development north of Mombasa, there are a few places in this area where campers are welcomed.

Access
Car   Between Mombasa and Malindi a good tar road (the B8) runs parallel to the coast a few kilometres inland. Most of the campsites are on the beach, and consequently a short distance off the main road.
Bus/Hitch   Frequent buses and matatus run between Mombasa and Malindi. To hitch out of Mombasa towards any of the campsites on the north coast, the best place is at the New Nyali Bridge toll booths about 3km from the city centre.

There are five campsites on this stretch of the coast.

SEAWAVES COTTAGES, Bamburi Beach
Formerly called The Coraldene Hotel, this site has a hotel block, a bar/restaurant, and some thatched cottages overlooking the hotel's private beach. Sailboards can be hired.

Position   10 km north of Mombasa on main Mombasa – Malindi road. Huge quarry and cement works on left. Turn right down dirt road (signposted) for 0.5 km.
Cost   50/– ppn.
Facilities   Camping is allowed on a patch of ground behind the cottages. Thorns stick up through the uncut grass, and the toilets and showers are as run-down as the rest of the place. Campers are allowed to use bathrooms in unoccupied cottages. The restaurant provides beers, meals and music.

Opposite Seawaves is **Bamburi Quarry**. Part of the old workings have been transformed by a rehabilitation scheme. The rehabilitation area and the Baobab Farm Nature Trail are open to the public. The ravaged landscape has been transformed into a remarkable profusion of trees and wildlife.

JUMBA LA MATWANA RUINS, Mtwapa
The ruins of an ancient Swahili town, with grand houses, mosques and wells. Now a national monument, this is an interesting site, more low-key than Gedi, further up the coast. Additional entertainment is provided by monkeys and hornbills in the huge old baobab trees that loom over the ruins.

The Jumba National Monument is open 0830 − 1830 h.
Entrance Fees: Non-resident 50/− (children/student 10/−), Resident 5/− (3/−).
  The campsite is a grassy area beneath trees next to the picnic site between the beach and the ruins. Swimming is good at high tide.

Position   From Mombasa on the B8, turn right 1 km north of Mtwapa Bridge. From Malindi turn left 36.5 km south of the Kilifi Ferry. The ruins are well signposted 3 km down a good murram road.
Cost   20/− ppn (plus site entrance fee on the first night).
Facilities   The picnic site has tables and benches. The very clean toilets and showers are near the ticket office, which means a spooky three minute scuttle back through the ruins after dark. The office sells cold sodas, but for basic foods the nearest dukas are on the murram road between ruins and the main road, or at Mtwapa.
Security   No askari, but there have been no reports of any trouble. Yet.

KANAMAI CONFERENCE AND HOLIDAY CENTRE/YOUTH HOSTEL, Kanamai

This centre is owned and managed by the National Council of Churches and caters mainly for Kenyan groups. Individuals and tourists are welcome though and the centre is also an official IYHF youth hostel. Camping is not allowed on the nearby beach.

Position   From Mombasa on the B8 turn right in Majengo 4 km north of Mtwapa Bridge. From Malindi, Majengo is 33.5 km south of the Kilifi ferry. From Majengo it is 3 km on dirt road to Kanamai.
The centre vehicle goes to Mombasa for supplies leaving every Tuesday and Friday at 0730 h and returning around 1300 h.
Cost   20/− ppn.
Facilities   Toilet and shower blocks, equipped kitchen (5/− ppn extra), common room, shop on site, canteen.
Security   Fenced on three sides (open to the beach), askaris, lights. Gear can be stored in the reception office.
Dormitories   40/− ppn (30/− ppn to IYHF members).

Near Kanamai observant campers may notice a sign to 'SN Cottages and Camping'. It seems this site no longer exists.

CONTINENTAL BEACH COTTAGES, Kikambala

A self-catering cottage complex overlooking the beach. Smart and well-organised and, although not specifically designed for camping, the management allow tents to be pitched on the shady lawn, either near the pool or in a more secluded spot behind the cottages.

Position From Mombasa turn right 4.5 km beyond Mtwapa Bridge, signposted to Whispering Palms Hotel. Continue 2.5 km down dirt road to Cottages.

Cost 50/- ppn.

Facilities Clean showers and toilets, bar, restaurant, swimming pool (30/- extra). Wood fires are not permitted. The nearest duka is opposite Whispering Palms Hotel 0.5 km south on the track, or in the EAP Church compound further on.

Security High fence, askaris.

KIKAMBALA BEACH COTTAGES, Kikambala

Another set of self-catering cottages on the beach. Not as smart but more homely than their Continental neighbours. A shady grassy area has been set aside for camping.

Position As for Continental Cottages above.

Cost 20/- ppn (high season), 15/- ppn (low season).

Facilities Pit toilet, basic shower. You can use the bar at the Continental Beach Cottages next door.

Security Fence, lights, askaris, and guard dogs with wagging tails that sum up the friendly atmosphere.

The new Mombasa Marine National Park has recently been gazetted north of Mombasa, between Bamburi and Shanzu beaches.

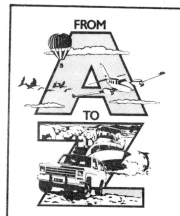

MALINDI

Malindi was one of a group of independent Swahili city-states, established along the coast long before the Portuguese were the first Europeans to visit the East African shoreline. During British colonial times it was a popular holiday spot, and more recently the town has developed into a full-blown seaside resort for Kenyan residents and tourists from many different countries. Malindi now boasts luxury hotels, ice-cream shops, souvenir stalls and even a pizza parlour.

Despite the development Malindi is still an attractive town. Being geographically between Mombasa and Lamu, it seems to come somewhere halfway on atmosphere as well. Malindi is far less hectic than Mombasa, but it could never be compared with laid back Lamu.

A range of hotels caters for all budgets and Malindi also has a youth hostel, but beds are often hard to come by in the high season.

There is one campsite on the outskirts of town, and another at Watamu, 20 km to the south.

Access

Car Malindi is 120 km north of Mombasa. The road is tarred all the way. The vehicle ferry at Kilifi carries cars free of charge, although you may have to queue for a while.

Bus/Hitch Many buses run between Mombasa and Malindi each day. Hitching along this road is no problem.

SILVERSANDS CAMPSITE

A popular and well-established campsite in a beautiful setting overlooking the sandy beach and coral reef beyond. Short grass runs right down to the sand and palm trees help create create a Pacific Ocean atmosphere. The site's only disadvantage is its popularity; at times it can get very crowded.

Swimming at high tide is excellent, and if you're feeling active Silversands hire out bicycles and organise snorkelling trips to the Watamu Marine Park.

Position Silversands is about 2 km south of Malindi town beach along the coast road, or a 2.5 km walk from the bus station. Robberies are not uncommon along this stretch of road, so walking alone, or in small groups, at night, is not advised. Take a taxi, 30/−.

Cost 30/−ppn (children under 10, 10/−; under 5, free)

Facilities Sinks, toilets and showers, all cleaned daily. Water is supplied by a mains link, with a back up from a reserve tank and private well. The site shop sells sodas, vegetables, bread, milk and tins. Meals and snacks are available at the restaurant.

Security The site is lit at night, and guarded by two askaris. However despite all efforts by the management some cases of theft still occur.

Bandas A variety of huts priced between 120/− and 220/− per double. Costs decrease the longer you stay.

The Driftwood Club, 10 mins south along the beach, provides the nearest beer, swimming pool, windsurfing and scuba diving. Temporary day membership is required to use the facilities.

The Youth Hostel, 1 km from the town centre/bus station, offers dormitories and the usual facilities. Sleeping on the roof is allowed and free-standing tents could be erected by determined campers in the event of monsoons! Cost: 35/- ppn.

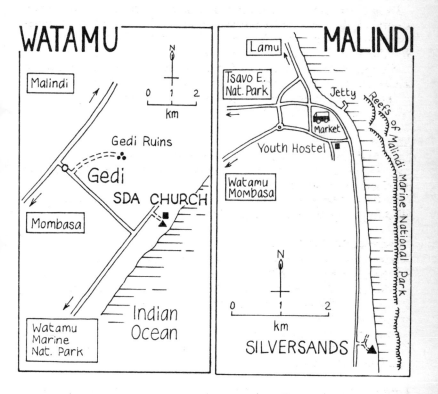

SEVENTH DAY ADVENTIST CHURCH, Watamu

Watamu is on the coast 20 km by road south of Malindi, originally a small fishing village but today the small collection of huts and dukas are now completely surrounded by a line of villas and holiday-homes extending along the beach. Some large hotels and accompanying touristy restaurants complete the scene.

The SDA Church is a mission centre with a dispensary and nursery school. A guest house and some bandas are available for rent and there is a patch of ground for camping. Although it provides an important service for the local community, the place is very dilapidated. Its only saving grace is the position on low cliffs overlooking the horse-shoe of Watamu Bay.

Officially, reservations must be made at the SDA Church Head-quarters, East African Union, PO Box 42276, Nairobi, Tel: 566025/520927, but are not usually necessary. A glance at the visitors book shows few people stay in the bandas or house, and even fewer camp. The most regular guests appear to be units of the British Army on 'rest & recuperation'.

Position Leave the main B8 Mombasa – Malindi road at Gedi, and follow the road for 4 km to Watamu. Turn left at the T-junction and the SDA Church is 1 km on the right. There are occasional matatus to Watamu; wait at the Gedi junction. The roads are tarred all the way.

Cost 35/– ppn.
Facilities Communal showers and toilets (really communal!). Filthy, no privacy and seldom water.
Security Uncertain.
Bandas 55/– ppn. *Guest House* 75/– ppn.

Just off the road between Malindi and Wataumu, **Gedi Ruins** are the remains of a once great Swahili settlement, with an impressive selection of houses, mosques and shops. Still surrounded by the dense forest that hid the site for many centuries Gedi has an evocative 'lost city' atmosphere.

Further from Malindi, about 40 km to the north, **The Marafra Depression** is the remains of a huge sandstone ridge that has been deeply eroded by rain. It is now a gorge scarred with steep gulleys and gashes, and a series of narrow edges branching out from the main gorge wall to end in small peaks and needles. The exposed sandstone strata ranges from brilliant white through bright pinks and crimsons to deep orange. We were told that the place is known locally as Nyari, or 'the place broken by itself'. An apt description.

It is possible to spend a couple of hours exploring the Marafra Depression, or, if you're completely self-contained with tent, gear and water, it would be an excellent place to camp wild for a day or two.

The best time to see the Marafra Depression is in the evening when the setting sun highlights the colours of the sandstone. With a car Marafra makes a good day's outing, and you can still get back to Malindi before dark if you need to. For travellers without a vehicle visiting Marafra involves a bus and matatu trip, and time-tabling virtually enforces an overnight stop. Camping above the Depression is unlikely to be dangerous, either due to erosion or thieves, but ask at the police station if unsure.

LAMU

Like Malindi, Mombasa and other ports and islands along the East African coastline, Lamu was once a powerful independent Swahili city-state. Built on an island, a short ferry ride from the mainland, 220 dusty kilometres north of Malindi, Lamu still retains an air of aloof remoteness in these more modern times.

This relaxed isolation made Lamu a popular hippy hangout in the early seventies, and more recently it has attracted fly-in package tourists and day-trippers from Mombasa. The beach is a huge windy expanse of sand, vastly over-hyped, and the Old Town streets see a growing number of tourist restaurants and souvenir shops every year, but the surrounding islands (if you can get to them) still manage to hang on to their charm, although if the planned American naval station is built here, the culture and way of life in all the Lamu group islands will probably be destroyed for ever.

Lamu offers a wide range of accommodation, from luxury hotels for the wealthy visitors to basic lodges with roof space for shoestring travellers. Until recently there was little in the way of camping but Said Abdullah Said of the Rainbow Guest House now has a campsite on the south side of Lamu town.

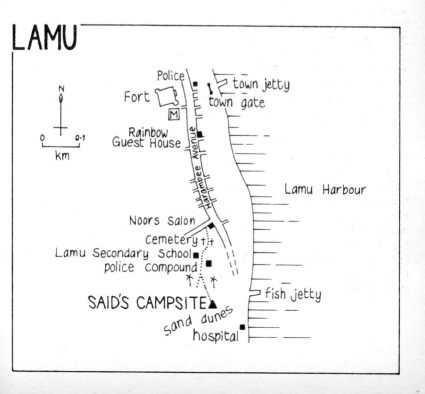

Access

Car   Very few car drivers bring their vehicles from Malindi to Lamu. It is a long hard drive on dirt roads to the ferry across to Lamu island, and as cars are not allowed on the island itself, a car would have to be left on the mainland anyway. All visitors are advised to fly from Malindi or Mombasa or take the bus.

Plane   Various private air companies fly planes daily between Mombasa, Malindi and Lamu (more in high season).

Bus/Hitch   Buses run daily between Malindi and the jetty for the ferry over to Lamu island. The ferry waits for the bus. Hitching has been known but takes a very long time.

SAID ABDULLAH SAID'S CAMPSITE

No name has yet been chosen for the new campsite, so visitors lost in Lamu's maze of streets and alleyways and asking for directions, should get put on the right track using this name. The campsite is on a small farm compound surrounded by palm trees and sand dunes. Rooms in the farm house are available for hire, and Said plans to have permanent tents on the site.

Position   To reach Said's Campsite from the main jetty follow the main street southwards (ie keep the sea to your left) past the Rainbow Lodge (you could check for directions here) turn right at Noor's Beauty Salon and bend to your left through the cemetery. Pass the police compound on your left and the secondary school on your right then bear left to reach Said's.

Cost   20/− ppn.

Facilities   Well water, toilets, showers.

Security   An old farmworker and his dog guard the site at night. (The site is near the police compound.)

House   40/− ppn in double rooms. Weekly and monthly stays negotiable.

Said organises a variety of distractions when the lure of the beach wanes, as do many other lodge owners and dhow sailors (find them down on the sea front), including dhow fishing trips, overnight excursions to nearby islands and, for the really adventurous, even elephant viewing...!

Information supplied by Matthew Rowntree (Britain).

SOUTH OF MOMBASA

South of Mombasa, beyond Likoni, are the two major resort centres of Tiwi Beach and Diani Beach. The beaches here are undeniably beautiful, but once again development has taken its toll and much of this scenic stretch of coastline is hidden behind concrete apartment blocks and high security fences. At Tiwi the development has been fairly low key, but at Diani it is almost out of control and in a few years this resort will be almost indistinguishable from the Greek Islands or the Costa del Sol.

Access
Car   Tiwi and Diani Beaches are both to the east of the main A14 Mombasa − Lunga Lunga road (tar). To reach this road from Mombasa it is necessary to cross the Likoni ferry.
Bus/Hitch   Most buses and matatus heading south down the main coast road depart from the south side of the Likoni ferry. This is also the best point to hitch if you are heading south.

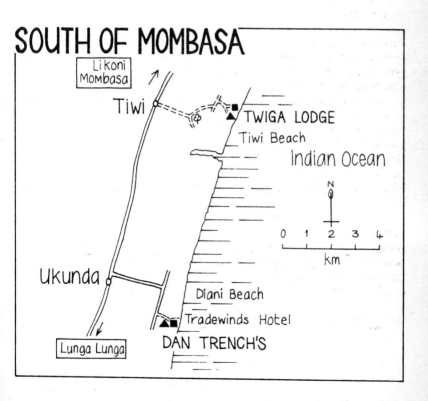

TWIGA LODGE, Tiwi Beach

Twiga Lodge and Campsite is in a fine position on an old coral platform overlooking the sea. Huge trees provide shade but the grass is patchy. Twiga Lodge is very popular and can be crowded, especially at holiday times (Christmas and Easter) when residents as well as tourists make for the coast. Overland trucks use the site too, so don't expect seclusion, expect a party. Swimming is good at high tide. An old mosque and fishing villages can be reached at low tide by walking along the beach, although security may be dubious.

Position Tiwi is 18 km south of the Likoni ferry on the A14. Tiwi beach is 3 km east of the main road. Twiga Lodge is signposted at this junction. The A14 is tarred, and the dirt road to the beach is suitable for all vehicles, although care is needed on the last 50 m down to the campsite.
   No public transport runs between the main road and the beach. Armed thuggery is an ever-increasing problem on this track, so hitch, do not walk, even in a group.
Cost 20/−ppn.
Facilities Plenty of water, cold showers, toilets usually clean except towards the end of the day. Firewood is available. Beer and meals at the lodge next to the campsite. Snorkel and flipper hire.
Security Fence, askaris, lights. Watch the monkeys!

DAN TRENCH'S, Diani Beach

Dan Trench's is the only campsite at package-tourist orientated Diani Beach. Dan comes from an old Kenya family and the campsite is in the back garden of his house, standing alone, virtually surrounded by hotels and clubs.
   The campsite is grassy and shady and has always been a popular place. It is now leased from Dan by New Zealander Richard Hewitt of Therion Safaris, Nairobi.
   You get to the beach along a path beside the Tradewinds Hotel.

Position The turn-off to Diani Beach is 25 km south of the Likoni ferry, just north of Ukunda. From the junction it's 2.5 km to the Diani beach road. Turn right and Dan Trench's is 1 km on the left. Look for the Tradewinds signpost as there is no sign to Dan Trench's.
Frequent buses run from Likoni to Ukunda. The number 32 loops up and down the beach road past Tradewinds.
Cost 30/- ppn; fixed tents 40/- ppn. Beds 50/- ppn.
Facilities Water, toilets, showers.
Security Security lights and high fence, 24 hour security guard service. Big (rucksack size) lockers for hire.
Bookings/Enquiries Therion Safaris, 3rd Floor, Data Centre Building, Kenyatta Ave, Nairobi. PO Box 70559; Tel: 24998/20317.

Security There is none, and theft is common. Gear can be locked in the small hut during the day, if you hire the hut. The big dormitory hut gives little security as 'pole-fishers' hook stuff out through the air-holes in the walls.

NOTE Dan Trench says that if he sells his home and land, a condition of sale will be the continuation of the campsite.

Shell collecting is a big problem on this stretch of the coast. The reefs are being destroyed for souvenirs. Coral is a living thing, do not kill it.

It seems that the guards at Twiga Lodge have got the security situation well covered. Early in the evening they can be seen diligently patrolling the campsite armed with torches and bows and arrows. If you have to visit the toilet in the night though, be careful where you step; you're quite likely to trip over one of the guards asleep at the foot of a tree!

Having said that, Twiga Lodge must be one of the best campsites on the coast. It's in an idyllic position and the chances of anything being stolen are far less than at Silversands or Dan Trench's. We'd driven from Nairobi to the coast, mostly off road through Tsavo West, and Twiga was a great place to rest up for a while. (Alistair and Pauline Taylor, Australia and Britain)

WASINI ISLAND

Wasini is a small island off the southern tip of the Shimoni Peninsula about 80 km south of Mombasa. The island supports an old Muslim community, developed in semi-isolation from the mainland, and has only received visitors in the last ten years or so, after a great deal of dissent among certain members of the community who did not want Wasini to become a second Lamu. This is unlikely as the island would have great difficulty supporting an increased population, albeit transient, as it has no permanent water supply, relying totally on rainfall which is collected and stored in large concrete tanks. So to date Wasini Island still has a remote and unspoilt feel to it.

Access

Car Wasini Island can be reached by ferry from the village of Shimoni, 80 km south of Mombasa's Likoni ferry. Follow the main A14 Mombasa – Lunga Lunga road and turn left onto a dirt road 1 km after Ramisi. From this junction to Shimoni is 15 km.

Bus/Hitch At least one bus per day runs between Mombasa and Shimoni. Alternatively take a Mombasa – Lunga Lunga bus and walk or hitch from the Ramisi junction.

From Shimoni jetty a 'matatu-boat' chugs to both villages on the island, Mskwiri and Wasini. This costs 35/– return, after heavy negotiation (Locals pay 5/– or 10/–). A dug-out canoe makes a shaky journey for 20/–, tides permitting.

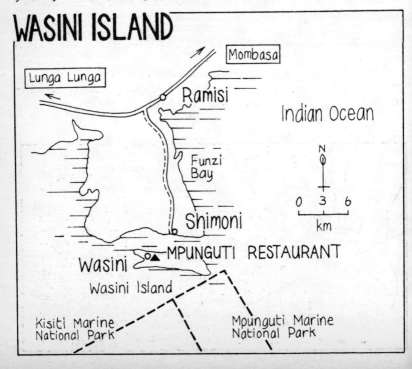

WASINI ISLAND

MPUNGUTI RESTAURANT AND CAMPSITE

In Wasini village a local man named Masoud Abdullah has built a campsite on low grassy cliffs looking back towards Shimoni. A big baobab tree provides a barrier from the blistering sun, and a pleasantly airy white-washed Swahili restaurant in the compound gives another retreat. Masoud also rents out huts and likes to encourage visitors to partake of his excellent coconut-with-everything Swahili meals.

Position   You can see Mpunguti Campsite on the cliffs to your left as you come into Wasini on the ferry. It's a minutes walk after landing.
Cost   20/− ppn.
Facilities   Pit toilet and bucket shower. The necessary water allowance given to visitors means that these must be used sparingly.
Security   Askaris are not necessary, because in this isolated strictly Muslim area thefts are literally unknown. *Insh'allah*, long may it remain this way.
Huts   250 − 300/− full board double, price varies seasonally.

The nearest beer is 10 minutes walk away at **Wasini Island Restaurant** (the only evidence of mass tourism on the island), where you can also book a visit to the Marine Park on a dhow for 350/− inclusive. It is possible for groups of up to six people to hire local boats at 1000/− per boat, but some people have been disappointed when confronted with a dug-out canoe, leaking masks, and half a flipper.

Remember that Wasini is a traditional Muslim community so don't go baring all under the sun.

Behind Wasini village are the strange **Coral Gardens**, statues of coral eroded from an ancient reef.

A boat ride away is **Kisiti Marine National Park** where the reefs are pristine, undamaged so far by thoughtless souvenir hunters, and the snorkelling reputed to be the best on the coast.

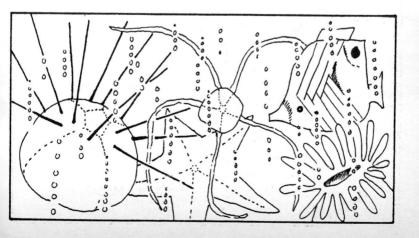

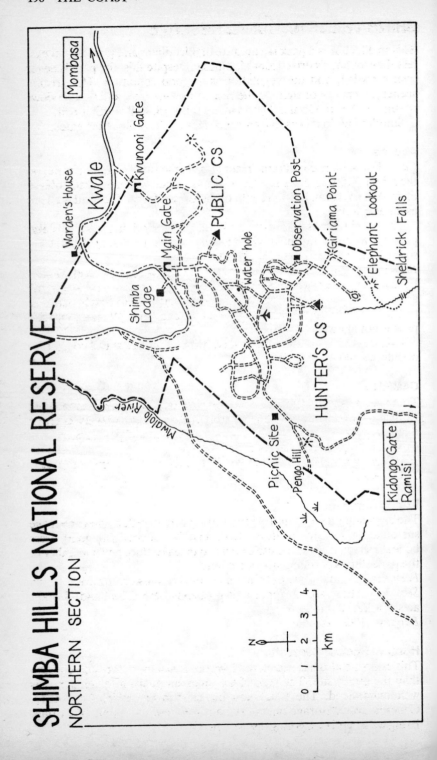

SHIMBA HILLS NATIONAL RESERVE
NORTHERN SECTION

Mombasa

Kwale

Warden's House

Kivunoni Gate

Main Gate

PUBLIC CS

Shimba Lodge

water hole

Observation Post

Giriama Point

Elephant Lookout

Sheldrick Falls

HUNTER'S CS

Mwalolo River

Picnic Site

Pengo Hill

Kidongo Gate
Ramisi

N

0 1 2 3 4
km

SHIMBA HILLS NATIONAL RESERVE

This small, compact park is a mixture of hilly plains and forested valleys, less than an hour's drive from Mombasa. Despite this, the park is never over-crowded, and the vegetation is in good condition. The pristine scenery, a chance of sighting the rare sable antelope, and superb views of sunrise over the Indian Ocean make this park well worth a visit.

Standard national reserve entrance fees are payable at the gates.

Access

Car   The main route into the reserve is via the small town of Kwale, on the minor C106 Ngombeni − Lunga Lunga road, which branches off the main A14 coast road 10 km south of the Likoni ferry. The road is tarred as far as Kwale.

The Main Gate is 3 km beyond Kwale on a good dirt road. It is also possible to enter the park via Kivunoni (eastern) Gate, about 1 km south of the C106 3 km before Kwale.

Bus/Hitch   Buses travel frequently between Mombasa and Kwale. Each day two buses go beyond Kwale to Kinango, passing the main gate and traversing part of the reserve. Although the road to Kwale is tarred, traffic is slight and hitching might take a long time. Walking into the park is not allowed.

Half-day safaris around the reserve with Mombasa travel companies cost about 300/−.

CAMPING

There is one special campsite, and one public campsite in the reserve. Both are in excellent settings and rarely visited. The special site is a little dilapidated, but the public site is well maintained and peaceful.

Cost   30/−ppn. Special campsites 300/− psw.

Booking   The Warden, Shimba Hills National Reserve, PO Box 16030, Kwale.

Public Campsite

The campsite is in a beautiful lofty setting with excellent views over the surrounding forested valleys. tents can be pitched on good grass beneath shady trees. This site also has bandas for hire and a member of the park staff is permanently based here.

Facilities   Pit toilet, water from tanks, bucket shower, firewood.

Security   There are no reports of problems here. The banda worker acts as askari if required.

Bandas   100/− double.

Hunters Special Campsite

This campsite also has excellent views but is in a more forested position than the public site. The lack of a permanent guard means it is not as well maintained. The toilet and bucket shower cubicles are dirty. Concrete water storage tanks exist but were empty at time of writing. Bring water and everything else you need.

Like most parks, walking *in to* the park is forbidden but walking *inside* the park, at certain points, is allowed. In Shimba the walk down to the impressive **Sheldrick Falls** takes about 45 minutes, but makes a pleasant diversion. Leave the track at Elephant Lookout and walk down the grassy slope to the forest at the bottom of the valley. Follow the path through the trees, over a small log bridge, through some small hillocks, then stay on the path as it bends to the left then drops steeply down to the foot of the falls. Before you go, though, remember that you are still in a national reserve and that large herds of buffalo and elephant inhabit the forest and drink at the pool below the falls. Take five minutes to check the forest from the appropriately named Elephant Lookout, and when you are walking make enough noise to warn any animals of your approach.

When we did this walk, a herd of elephants moved out of our way, leaving piles of fresh droppings and half chewed branches. We could smell them, but couldn't see far in the dense forest. When you're that close to large wild animals light conversation comes hard, so to let any other animals know we were on our way, we were reduced to singing snatches from half-remembered Gilbert and Sullivan songs. Whether it was the noise or the choice of song that kept the animals at bay I don't know, but we were able to reach the falls and return to the car without further adventure. (D.E., J.B.)

Index of Place Names

*(For other subjects see **Contents** page.)*

Aberdare Nat Park 129
Amboseli Nat Park 71-73
Archer's Post 158

Bamburi Quarry Nature Trail 183
Baragoi 150
Buffalo Springs Nat Res 157-159

Cherangani Hills 104-105
Chogoria 123

Dan Trench's 192

Eldoret 101
Eliye Springs 147
El Karama Ranch 139
Endebess 107

Ferguson's Gulf 147
Fourteen Falls 134

Gedi Ruins 188
Grogan's Castle 171

Hell's Gate Nat Park 80

Isiolo 161

Jumba La Matwana Ruins 183

Kakamega Forest 99-100
Kampi ya Samaki 88
Kapenguria 104
Kimilili 113
Kisiti Marine Nat Park 195
Kisumu 92-93
Kitale 102-104
Kubi Fora 163

Lake Baringo 88
Lake Bogoria Nat Park 85-87
Lake Chala 171
Lake Jipe 170
Lake Magadi 75
Lake Naivasha 79-80
Lake Nakuru Nat Park 83-84
Lake Turkana 146-147, 150-153
Lake Victoria 91, 92

Lamu 189-190
Likoni 180
Lodwar 146
Londiani 94-96
Loyangalani 152-153

Maasai Mara Nat Res 65-69
Malindi 186-188
Maralal 148-149
Marafra Depression 188
Marigat 85, 88
Marsabit Nat Park 161-162
Masara 107, **113**
Mathews Range 154-155
Mbita 93, 97
Mount Elgon Nat Park 107-108
Mount Elgon wild camping 109-115
Mount Kenya Nat Park 120-127
Meru Nat Park 141-143
Mfangano Island 93-94
Mombasa 180
Mrs Roche's 57
Mtito Andei 169

Nairobi 21, 40, **55-61**
Namanga 74
Nanyuki 137
Naro Moru 121
Nyahururu 135
Nyeri 129

Ol Doinyo Sapuk Nat Park 133
Olorgasailie Prehist Site 75

Robert's Camp 89
Rumuruti 136

Saiwa Swamp Nat Park 103
Samburu Highlands 148
Samburu Nat Res 157-159
Siaya 97-98
Sibiloi Nat Park 163-164
Silversands 186
Sirikwa Safaris 103
Sheldrick Falls 198
Shimba Hills Nat Res 197-198
Shimoni 194
South Horr 151

Soy 101-102

Thomson's Falls 135
Tsavo East Nat Park 173-175
Tsavo West Nat Park 169-171

Twiga Lodge 192

Voi 173, 177

Wasini Island 194-195

About the authors

David Else started life on the road on the back of his parent's tandem. He soon progressed to travelling independently in Britain, then Europe and eventually to Africa. Since 1983 he has spent more time in 'The Dark Continent' than in his own country, working and travelling all over Africa.

He regularly contributes to guide-books, magazines and journals. *Camping Guide to Kenya* is his fourth book published by Bradt Publications.

Back in Britain, when he isn't grappling with a word-processor or otherwise occupied with a grubby note-book and pen, David Else spends his time cycling, walking and climbing. He still can't afford a decent car, and to satisfy his lingering wanderlust he seems to spend most of his time travelling up and down motorways between Matlock in Derbyshire, London and South Wales.

Jill Bitten also had an early introduction to the world of independent travel, pedestrian camping around Wales with her parents.

She has travelled with David Else on many epic journeys through Europe and Africa, recording events on the back of envelopes with a blotchy ink pen.

Back at home, when she isn't on the end of a climbing rope, or fiddling with the car, Jill Bitten draws the maps, rearranges the words, and fills up the white spaces.